# Marching to the Table

## The Little Women Cookbook

The Little Women Cookbook
Autumn Rosewood
Copyright © 2025 by Autumn Rosewood
All rights reserved. No part of this book may be reproduced, stored in a retrieval system, or transmitted in any form or by any means—electronic, mechanical, photocopying, recording, or otherwise—without the prior written permission of the author, except in the case of brief quotations embodied in critical reviews and certain other noncommercial uses permitted by copyright law.

First Edition: January, 2025

This book is inspired by the novel Little Women by Louisa May Alcott. It is a tribute to the characters and stories within and does not claim to be affiliated with or endorsed by the original author's estate or publishers.

All recipes and photographs are the original creations of the author unless otherwise stated.

For inquiries, please contact:
AutumnRosewoodBooks@gmail.com
www.autumnrosewood.com


ISBN: 9798308042341
Printed in USA

# Table of Contents

Introduction
The March Family's Kitchen: A Window into Victorian Cooking
Adapting 19th-Century Recipes for the Modern Cook
Essential Ingredients and Tools of the Era

**Chapter 1: Morning at Plumfield**
Popovers with Strawberry Jam
Jo's Rustic Cornmeal Porridge
Meg's Buttermilk Pancakes
Honey-Glazed Ham and Biscuits
Victorian Fried Apples with Spices
Maple Syrup Johnny Cakes
Cranberry Orange Muffins

**Chapter 2: Luncheons and Light Meals**
Cucumber and Watercress Tea Sandwiches
Creamy New England Clam Chowder
Spinach and Bacon Salad with Warm Dressing
Victorian Chicken Salad
Rose Petal Lemonade
Pickled Limes

**Chapter 3: Hearty Suppers**
Mrs. March's Roast Beef with Pan Gravy
Succotash: A Classic New England Side
Colonial Chicken Pot Pie
Jo's Rustic Vegetable Stew
Baked Fish with Herbs and Lemon
Buttery Mashed Turnips and Potatoes

# Table of Contents

**Chapter 4: Sweet Treats and Desserts**
Apple Pandowdy
Blueberry Buckle with Crumb Topping
Meg's Molasses Cookies
Cranberry Cake with Warm Vanilla Sauce
Concord Grape Jam Tarts
Gingerbread Cake with Whipped Cream

**Chapter 5: Festive Feasts and Celebrations**
Thanksgiving Turkey with Sage Stuffing
Cranberry Sauce with Orange Zest
Christmas Honey-Glazed Ham
Fourth of July Berry Trifle
New Year's Eve Wassail Punch
Easter Hot Cross Buns

**Chapter 6: Tea Time Delights**
Classic Victoria Sponge Cake
Raspberry Thumbprint Cookies
Devonshire Cream Scones
Amy's Rose Petal Jam
Savory Cheese and Chive Biscuits
Earl Grey Tea Loaf

# Table of Contents

**Chapter 7: Preserves and Pantry Staples**
Concord Grape Jelly
Pickled Vegetables: A Taste of Preservation
Spiced Pear Butter
Amy's Fancy Lemon Curd

**Chapter 8: Everyday Comforts**
Chicken and Dumplings
Hearty Beef Stew with Root Vegetables
Potato and Leek Soup
Baked Macaroni with Cheese Crust
Shepherd's Pie with Herbed Mash
Warm Apple Cider with Cinnamon

# Introduction

When I think of Little Women, I'm always struck by the warmth and heart of the March family. Louisa May Alcott wrote a story that's so much more than its plot—it's a world filled with love, sacrifice, and small moments that mean everything. One of the ways that world feels so alive is through food. Whether it's the burnt popovers Jo tries to master, the elegant blancmange Meg prepares for Laurie, or the Christmas breakfast the sisters give away to a struggling family, food is woven into the story as a symbol of care and connection.

That's what inspired me to create this cookbook. I wanted to bring those flavors and moments to life—not just as they might have been in the 19th century, but in a way that we can enjoy and share today. Cooking has always felt like a way to connect with others, and this book is my way of inviting you into the March family's kitchen.

## Bringing the March Family's Table to Life

Food plays such an important role in Little Women. It's tied to the values the March family holds dear—kindness, generosity, and the joy of sharing what you have. From the modest breakfasts that nourish their bodies to the grander feasts that mark holidays and milestones, meals in the story feel personal and meaningful.

I've always loved imagining what it would have been like to sit at their table, to share in their laughter and stories. This cookbook is my attempt to bring that to life, to give us all a taste of the dishes that might have been served and to connect with the spirit of the March family.

## The March Family's Kitchen: A Window into Victorian Cooking

Victorian cooking was as much about resourcefulness as it was about flavor. The March family, living in Concord, Massachusetts, would have relied on local, seasonal ingredients—things like apples, cornmeal, and molasses were staples in their kitchen. Meals were often simple, made with care and without waste, yet still incredibly satisfying.

I love imagining their kitchen—a place where the sisters learned to cook, where mishaps turned into laughter, and where simple recipes carried the weight of love and effort. While we don't live in the same world today, there's something so special about bringing those values into our kitchens now. These recipes honor that spirit while being approachable for modern cooks.

## Adapting 19th-Century Recipes for the Modern Cook

When I started diving into the recipes of the 1800s, I realized how different cooking was back then. Instructions were vague, measurements were often approximate, and cooking equipment wasn't exactly what we're used to. A phrase like "bake until done" doesn't give much to work with!

For this cookbook, I've worked to adapt those recipes into something we can all recreate. I've updated the measurements, clarified the steps, and adjusted some ingredients for availability—but always with the goal of staying true to the original spirit. These recipes aren't about perfection; they're about care, effort, and the joy of sharing food with those you love.

## Essential Ingredients and Tools of the Era

The March family's kitchen wouldn't have been stocked with anything fancy, but they made the most of what they had. Some of the ingredients and tools I imagine them using are staples in my own kitchen today:

- Cornmeal and Molasses: Essentials for simple, hearty New England cooking.
- Fresh Apples: A versatile ingredient, perfect for pies, crisps, or even a plain snack.
- Dried Herbs: Parsley, thyme, and sage would have flavored many of their dishes.
- Cast Iron Skillet: A workhorse of the Victorian kitchen and just as essential now.
- Wooden Spoons and Stoneware Bowls: Practical and timeless tools.

You don't need a Victorian hearth or a churn to recreate these recipes—just a little curiosity and a love for good food. As you cook your way through these pages, I hope you feel connected to the March family's world and the warmth they shared.

So, let's get started! I hope this cookbook brings a little of that Little Women magic into your kitchen. Whether you're baking popovers, stirring a pot of stew, or enjoying a sweet plum pudding, I hope you feel the love and care that inspired these recipes. Happy cooking!

*Autumn Rosewood*

# Chapter 1: Morning at Plumfield

In Little Women, breakfast is a cherished time for the March family to gather around the table, sharing not only food but also stories and laughter. From Meg's delicate pancakes to Jo's hearty porridge, each dish reflects the comfort and warmth of home in Civil War-era New England. Join us as we start our day with a hearty New England breakfast inspired by the pages of Louisa May Alcott's beloved novel.

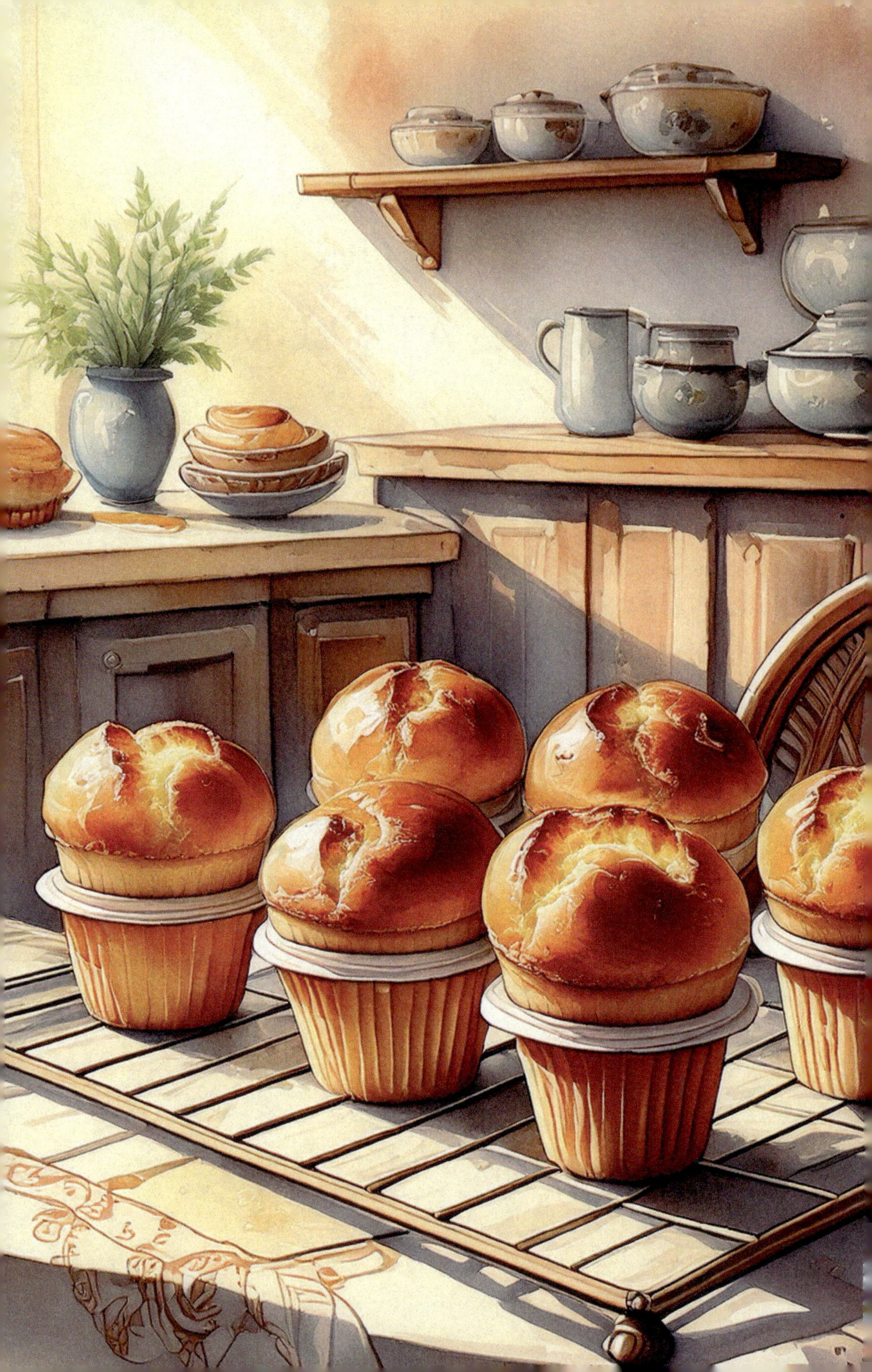

# Popovers with Strawberry Jam

Light, airy, and best served fresh from the oven, popovers are mentioned in Little Women when Jo struggles to master them. While her results were less than ideal, these popovers are guaranteed to rise beautifully. Pair them with strawberry jam for a perfect start to the day.

Ingredients:
- 2 large eggs, at room temperature
- 1 cup whole milk, at room temperature
- 1 cup all-purpose flour
- 1/4 teaspoon salt
- 1 tablespoon unsalted butter, melted (plus extra for greasing the pan)
- Strawberry jam or honey, for serving

Instructions:
1. Prepare the Pan: Preheat your oven to 450°F (230°C). Place a muffin tin or popover pan in the oven to heat while you prepare the batter.
2. Mix the Batter: In a medium bowl, whisk the eggs and milk together until well combined. Gradually add the flour and salt, whisking until smooth. Stir in the melted butter. The batter should have the consistency of heavy cream.
3. Carefully remove the hot pan from the oven and grease each cup with butter. Be generous to prevent sticking.
4. Fill the Cups: Pour the batter into the prepared cups, filling each about halfway. Work quickly to preserve the heat in the pan.
5. Bake for 20 minutes without opening the oven door. Reduce the temperature to 350°F (175°C) and bake for another 15–20 minutes, until the popovers are puffed and golden brown.
6. Serve: Remove from the oven and serve immediately with strawberry jam or honey. Popovers are best enjoyed fresh and hot.

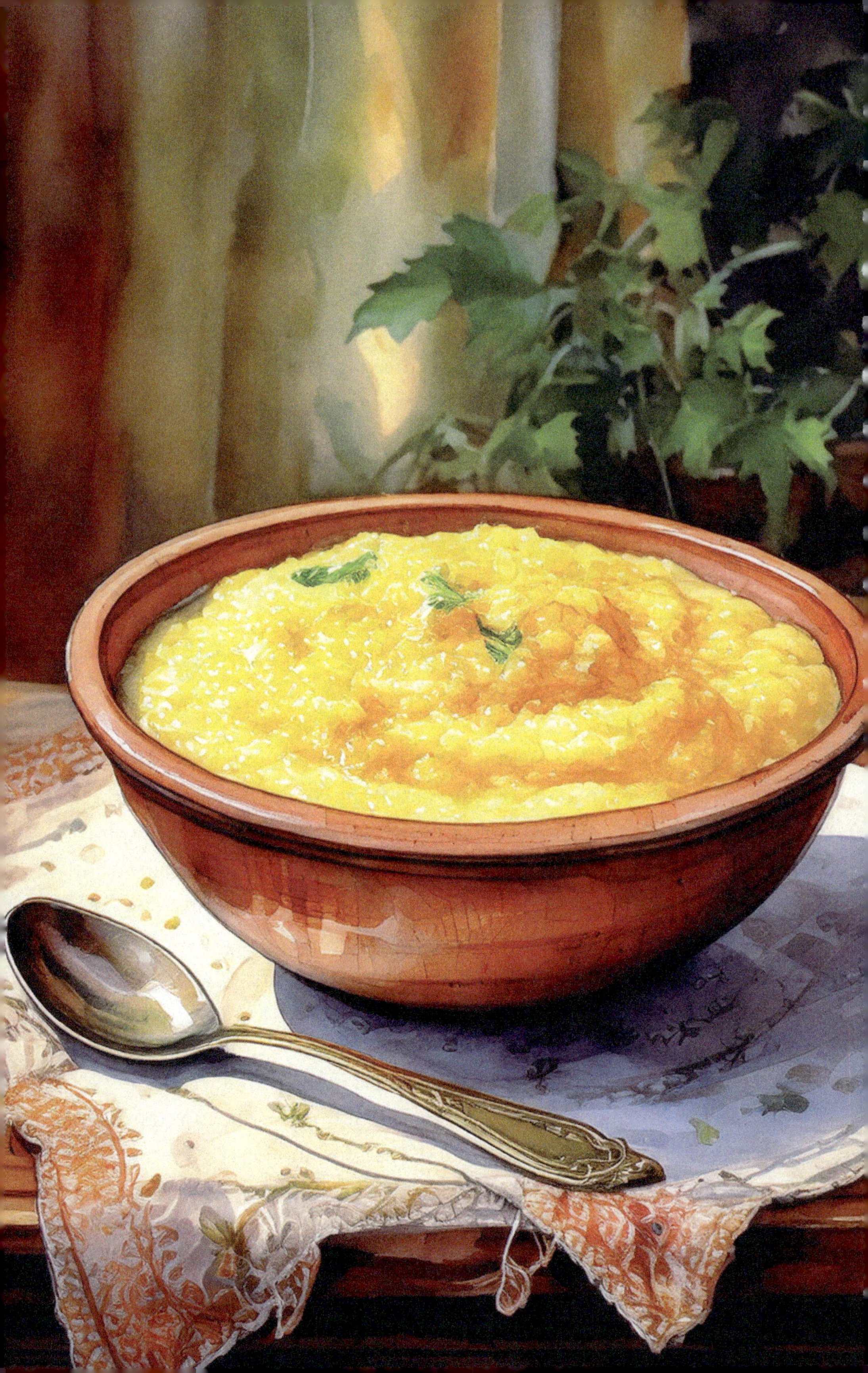

# Jo's Rustic Cornmeal Porridge

Jo's no-nonsense personality pairs well with this simple and hearty breakfast. Cornmeal porridge was a staple in New England, offering warmth and sustenance on busy mornings.

Ingredients:
- 1 cup yellow cornmeal
- 4 cups water
- 1/2 teaspoon salt
- 1/4 cup milk or cream (optional, for richness)
- Maple syrup, molasses, or butter, for serving

Instructions:
1. Prepare the Water: In a medium saucepan, bring the water and salt to a boil over medium-high heat.
2. Add the Cornmeal: Gradually whisk the cornmeal into the boiling water to avoid clumping. Reduce the heat to low.
3. Cook the Porridge: Stir the mixture frequently as it simmers for 15–20 minutes, or until the cornmeal is fully cooked and the porridge has thickened. Add a splash of milk or cream if desired for a richer texture.
4. Serve: Spoon the porridge into bowls and top with maple syrup, molasses, or a pat of butter for added flavor.

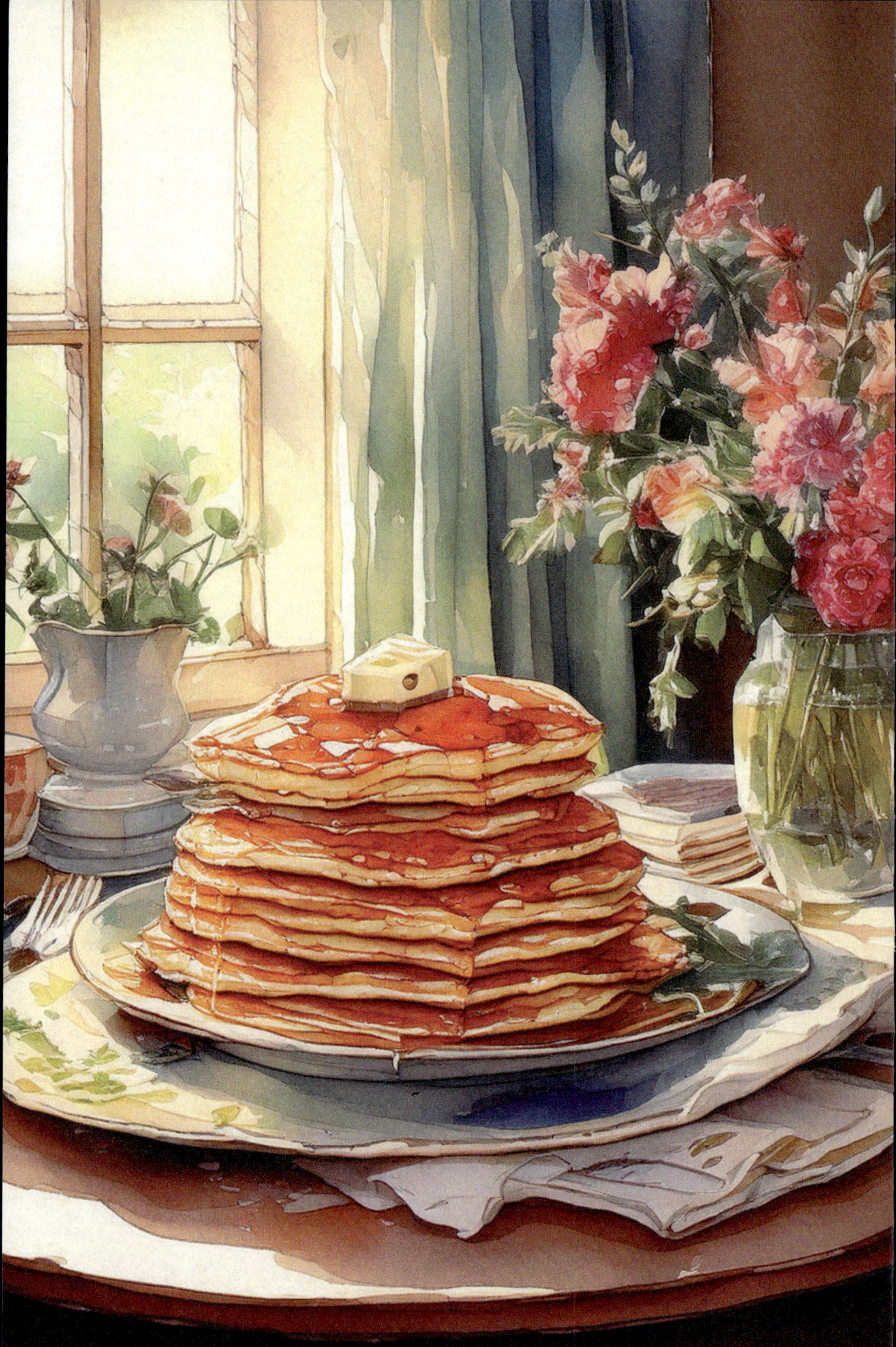

# Meg's Buttermilk Pancakes

Meg's nurturing spirit shines through in these tender and fluffy pancakes, perfect for bringing the family together at breakfast.

Ingredients:
- 1 cup all-purpose flour
- 2 tablespoons sugar
- 1 teaspoon baking powder
- 1/2 teaspoon baking soda
- 1/4 teaspoon salt
- 1 cup buttermilk
- 1 large egg
- 2 tablespoons unsalted butter, melted, plus more for cooking
- Butter and maple syrup, for serving

Instructions:
1. Prepare the Dry Ingredients: In a large bowl, whisk together the flour, sugar, baking powder, baking soda, and salt.
2. Combine Wet Ingredients: In another bowl, whisk the buttermilk, egg, and melted butter until smooth.
3. Mix the Batter: Pour the wet ingredients into the dry ingredients and gently stir until just combined. Do not overmix; a few lumps are fine.
4. Heat the Skillet: Heat a nonstick skillet or griddle over medium heat and lightly grease with butter.
5. Cook the Pancakes: Pour 1/4 cup of batter onto the skillet for each pancake. Cook until bubbles form on the surface and the edges look set, about 2–3 minutes. Flip and cook the other side until golden brown, another 1–2 minutes.
6. Serve: Keep the pancakes warm in a low oven if making in batches. Serve with butter and maple syrup.

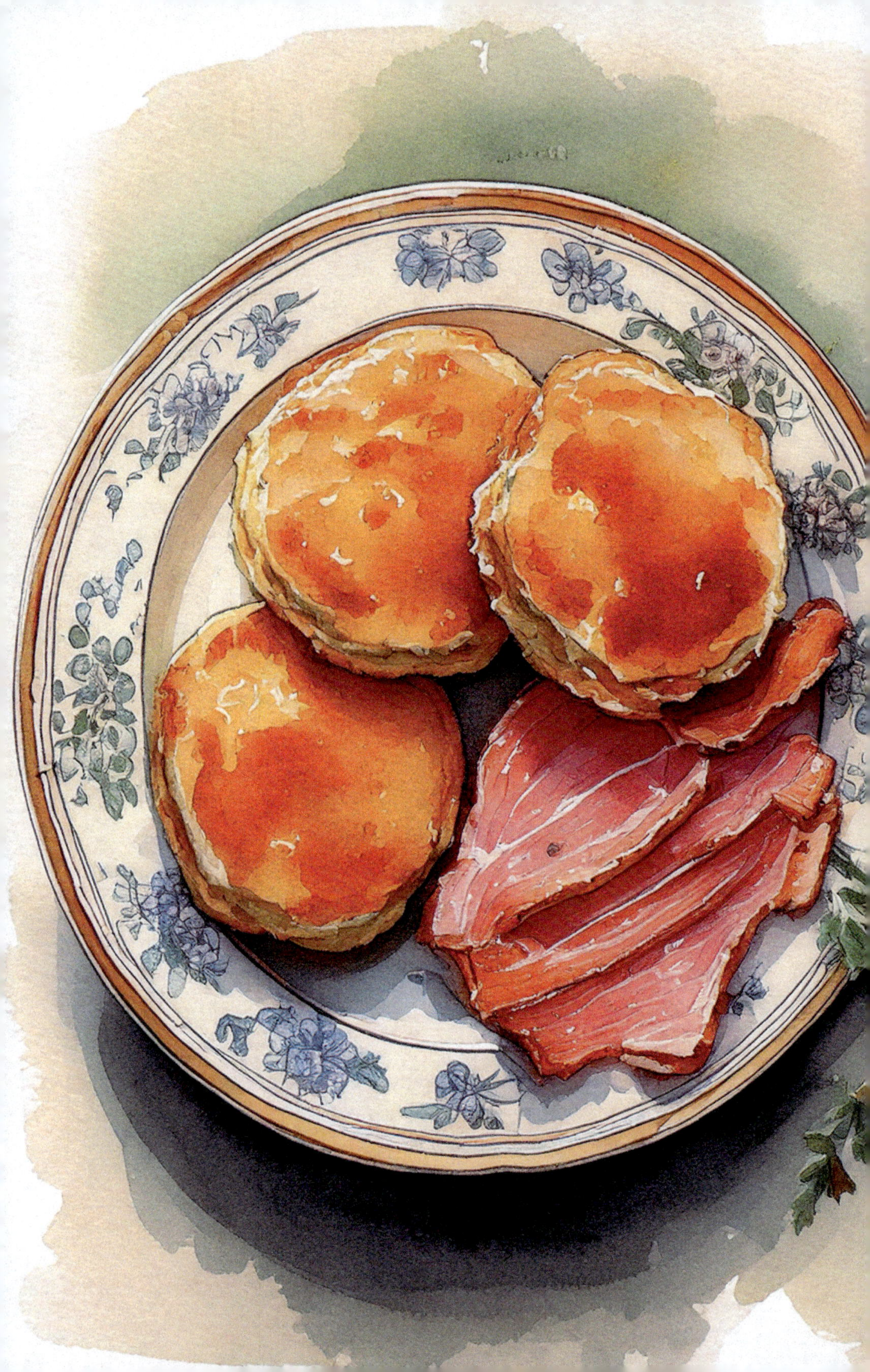

# Honey-Glazed Ham and Biscuits

This hearty breakfast pairs sweet and savory flavors, making it perfect for a special morning at Plumfield.

For the Ham:
- 1 small cooked ham steak (about 1 pound)
- 2 tablespoons honey
- 1 teaspoon Dijon mustard
- 1/4 teaspoon ground cloves

For the Biscuits:
- 2 cups all-purpose flour
- 1 tablespoon baking powder
- 1/2 teaspoon baking soda
- 1/2 teaspoon salt
- 1/4 cup unsalted butter, cold and cubed
- 3/4 cup buttermilk

Instructions for the Ham:
1. Prepare the Glaze: In a small bowl, mix the honey, mustard, and ground cloves.
2. Cook the Ham: Heat a skillet over medium heat. Brush the glaze on both sides of the ham steak and cook for 3–4 minutes per side, until heated through and caramelized.

Instructions for the Biscuits:

1. Preheat the Oven: Heat the oven to 425°F (220°C).
2. Combine Dry Ingredients: In a large bowl, whisk together the flour, baking powder, baking soda, and salt.
3. Cut in the Butter: Add the cubed butter and use a pastry cutter or your fingers to work it into the flour until the mixture resembles coarse crumbs.
4. Add the Buttermilk: Stir in the buttermilk just until the dough comes together.
5. Shape the Biscuits: Turn the dough out onto a floured surface and gently pat it to 1/2-inch thickness. Cut out biscuits using a round cutter or the rim of a glass.
6. Bake: Place the biscuits on a parchment-lined baking sheet and bake for 10–12 minutes, until golden brown.

Serve Together: Plate the ham slices alongside warm biscuits for a balanced, satisfying breakfast.

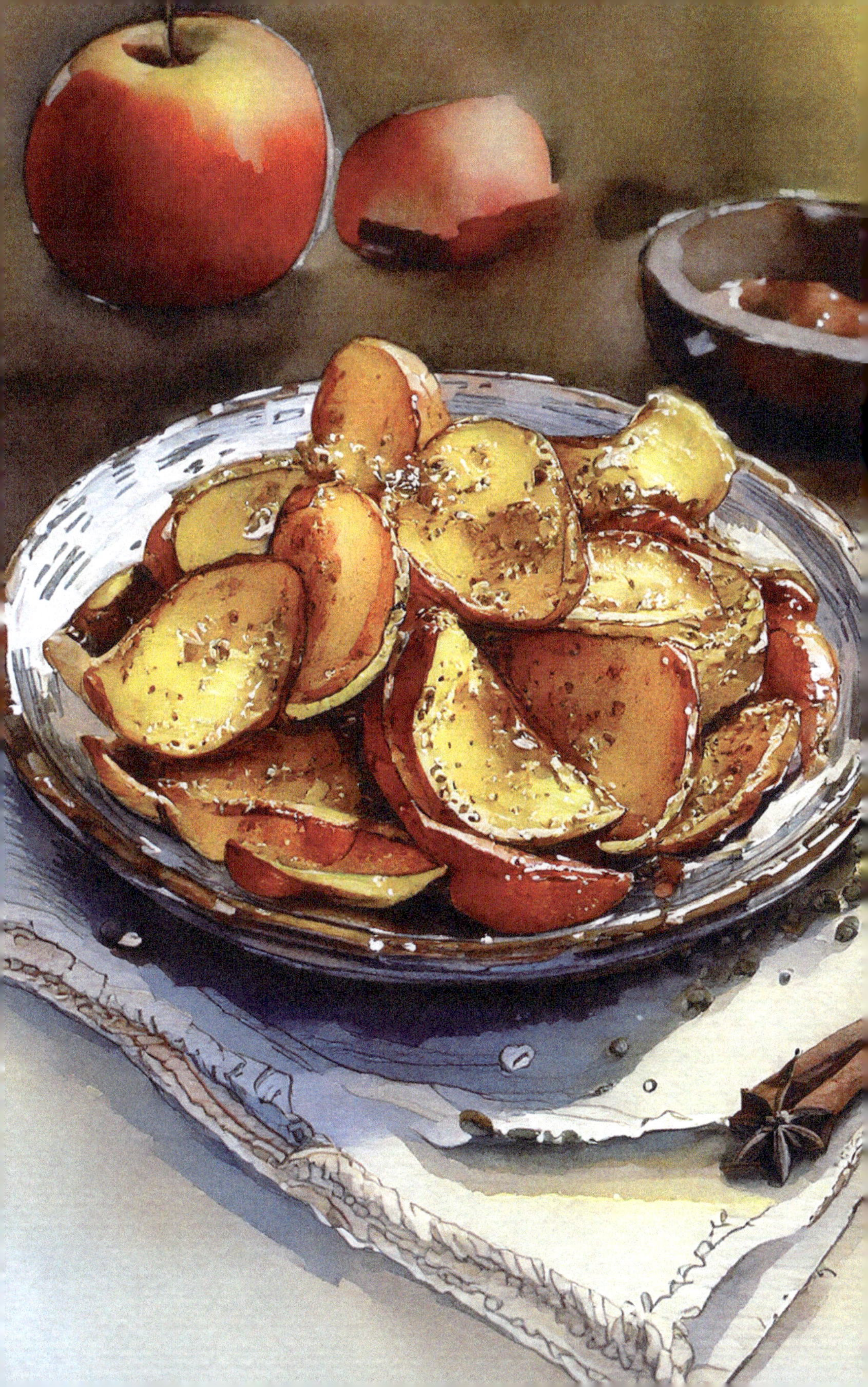

# Victorian Fried Apples with Spices

A warm and aromatic side dish, fried apples were a breakfast staple in New England homes. The lightly caramelized sweetness combined with a touch of spice makes them a cozy addition to any breakfast table.

Ingredients:
- 4 large apples (Granny Smith, Honeycrisp, or similar), peeled, cored, and sliced into 1/4-inch wedges
- 2 tablespoons unsalted butter
- 2 tablespoons brown sugar
- 1 teaspoon ground cinnamon
- 1/4 teaspoon ground nutmeg
- Pinch of ground cloves (optional)
- 2 tablespoons water
- Pinch of salt

Instructions:

1. Prepare the Apples: Slice the apples evenly to ensure they cook uniformly.
2. Heat the Butter: In a large skillet, melt the butter over medium heat until it begins to foam.
3. Cook the Apples: Add the apple slices to the skillet and sprinkle with brown sugar, cinnamon, nutmeg, cloves, and a pinch of salt. Stir to coat the apples evenly.
4. Simmer: Add 2 tablespoons of water to the skillet and cover. Reduce the heat to low and let the apples cook for 8–10 minutes, stirring occasionally, until they're tender but not mushy.
5. Caramelize: Remove the lid and cook for an additional 2–3 minutes to allow the liquid to reduce and lightly caramelize the apples.
6. Serve: Serve warm as a side dish, or spooned over pancakes or biscuits.

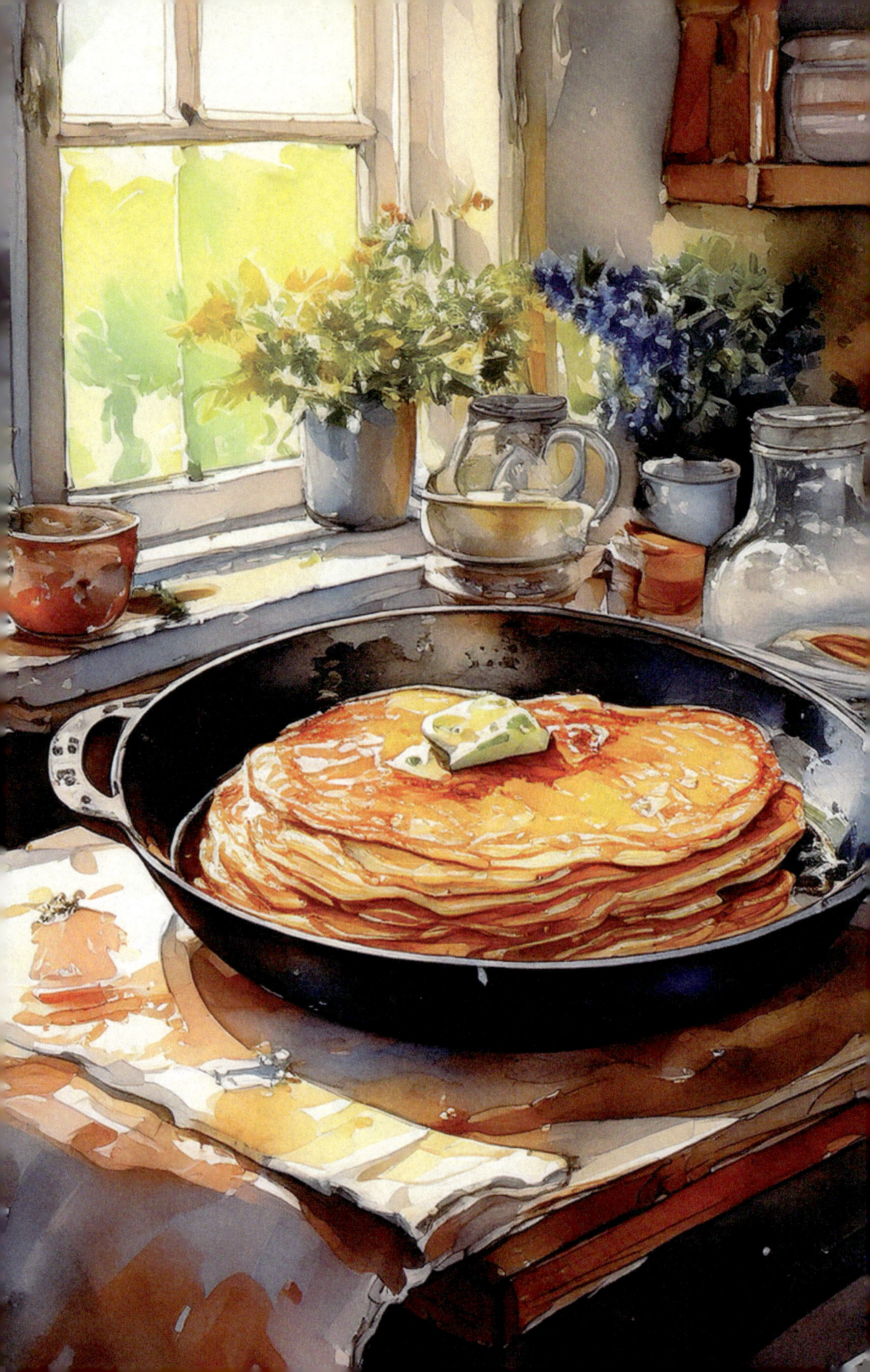

# Maple Syrup Johnny Cakes

Johnny cakes, made with cornmeal, were a New England classic and a staple in Victorian kitchens. This recipe captures the simplicity and heartiness of the dish, sweetened with a drizzle of maple syrup.

Ingredients:
- 1 cup yellow cornmeal
- 1 tablespoon sugar
- 1/2 teaspoon salt
- 1 cup boiling water
- 1/4 cup milk
- Butter, for greasing
- Maple syrup, for serving

Instructions:
1. Combine the Dry Ingredients: In a medium bowl, mix the cornmeal, sugar, and salt.
2. Add the Liquid: Gradually stir in the boiling water, whisking until smooth. Let the mixture cool slightly, then stir in the milk to create a thick batter.
3. Heat the Skillet: Heat a lightly greased cast-iron skillet or nonstick pan over medium heat.
4. Cook the Johnny Cakes: Drop spoonfuls of batter onto the skillet, flattening each slightly with the back of a spoon. Cook for 2–3 minutes on each side, until golden brown and crispy at the edges.
5. Serve: Serve warm with a generous drizzle of maple syrup.

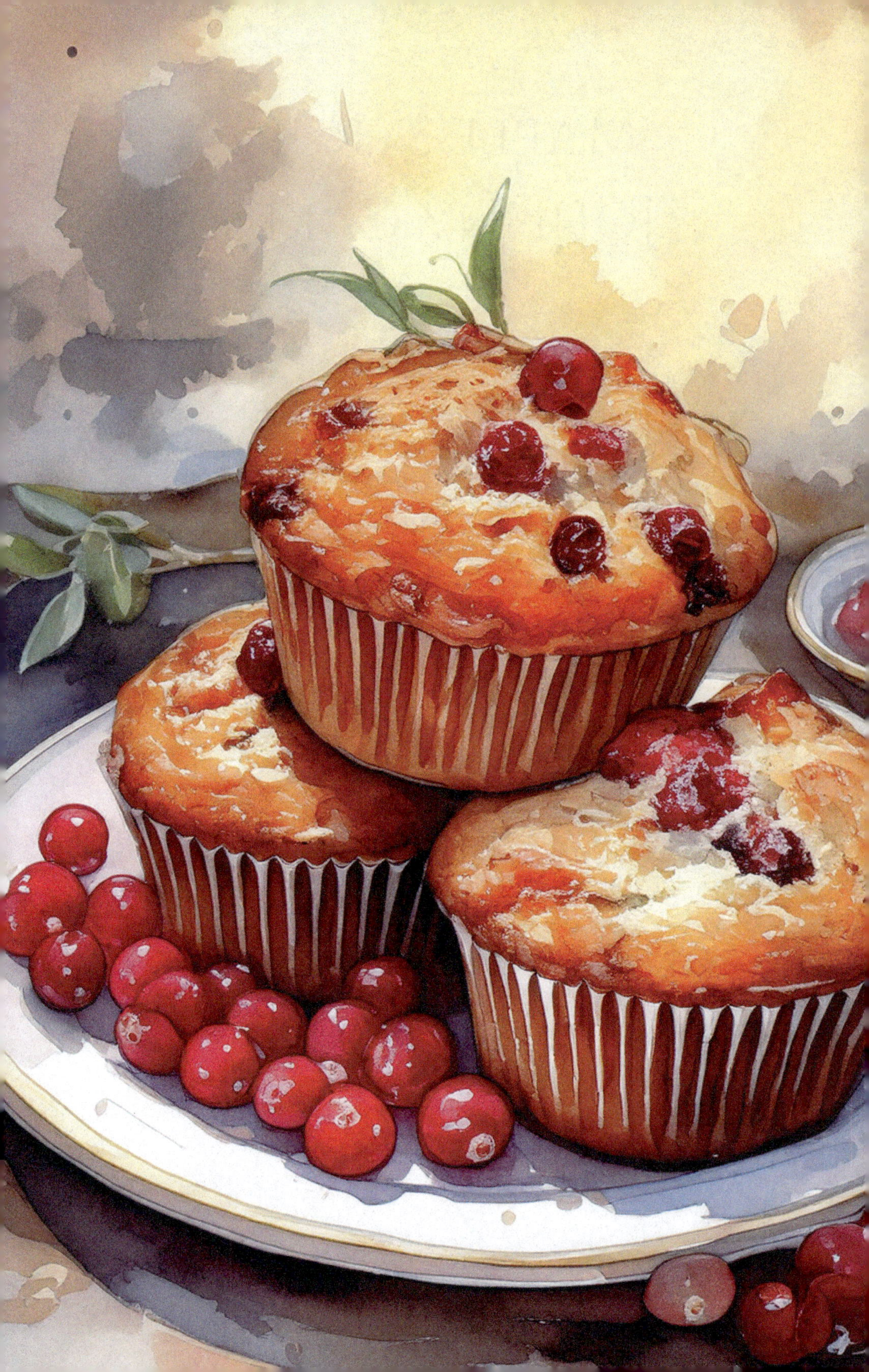

# Cranberry Orange Muffins

These muffins bring a bit of brightness to the breakfast table with their sweet and tangy flavor. Cranberries, a New England favorite, would have been a seasonal delight in the March family's kitchen.

Ingredients:
- 2 cups all-purpose flour
- 1 teaspoon baking powder
- 1/2 teaspoon baking soda
- 1/2 teaspoon salt
- 1/2 cup unsalted butter, softened
- 3/4 cup granulated sugar
- 2 large eggs
- 1 teaspoon vanilla extract
- Zest of 1 orange
- 1/2 cup orange juice
- 1 cup fresh or frozen cranberries, roughly chopped

Instructions:
1. Preheat the Oven: Preheat the oven to 375°F (190°C). Line a muffin tin with paper liners or grease with butter.
2. Mix the Dry Ingredients: In a medium bowl, whisk together the flour, baking powder, baking soda, and salt.
3. Cream the Butter and Sugar: In a large bowl, beat the butter and sugar until light and fluffy. Add the eggs one at a time, followed by the vanilla extract and orange zest.
4. Combine Wet and Dry Ingredients: Gradually add the dry ingredients to the wet mixture, alternating with the orange juice, starting and ending with the dry ingredients. Fold in the cranberries.
5. Fill the Muffin Tins: Divide the batter evenly among the muffin cups, filling each about 3/4 full.
6. Bake: Bake for 18–20 minutes, or until a toothpick inserted into the center comes out clean.
7. Cool and Serve: Let the muffins cool in the tin for 5 minutes before transferring them to a wire rack. Serve warm or at room temperature.

# Chapter 2: Luncheons and Light Meals

In Little Women, the midday meal is a time for reflection, connection, and sometimes even a touch of elegance. Whether it's a simple lunch enjoyed during a break from daily tasks or an elegant spread for a special gathering, these meals are full of charm and practicality. This chapter brings together recipes inspired by the March family's world, from Meg's refined tastes to Jo's hearty approach to food.

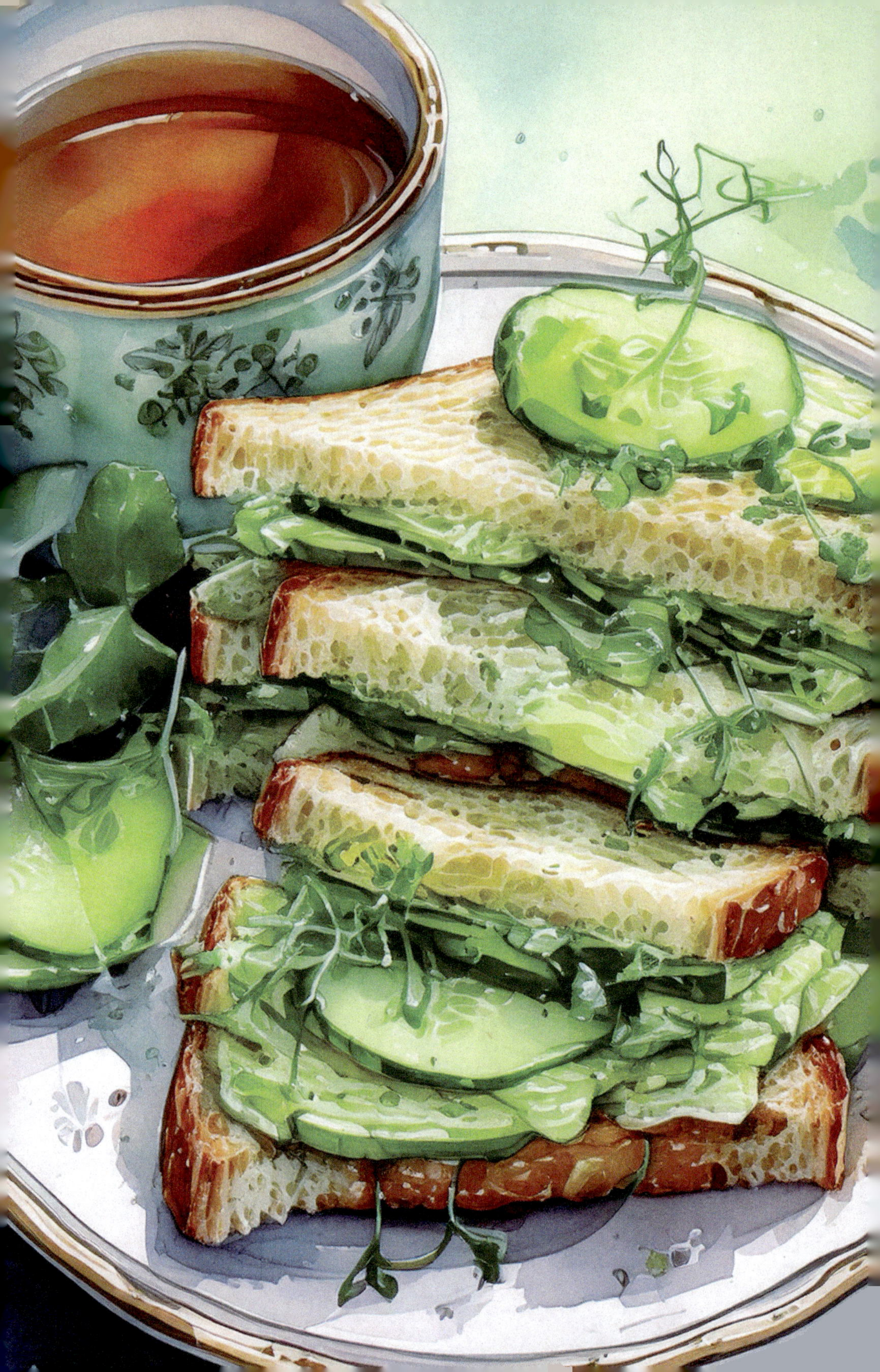

# Cucumber and Watercress Tea Sandwiches

These delicate tea sandwiches evoke the refined spirit of Meg, who would have proudly served them at one of her luncheons. They're simple yet elegant, perfect for a light meal or afternoon tea.

Serves: 4 (Makes 16 small sandwiches)

Ingredients:
- 8 slices of white or whole wheat bread, crusts removed
- 4 ounces cream cheese, softened
- 1 tablespoon fresh dill, finely chopped (optional)
- 1 English cucumber, thinly sliced
- 1 small bunch of watercress, stems removed
- Salt and freshly ground black pepper

Instructions:
1. Prepare the Bread: Lay the slices of bread flat and spread a thin, even layer of cream cheese on one side of each slice. If desired, mix the cream cheese with dill for added flavor.
2. Add the Filling: Arrange the cucumber slices in a single layer over half of the bread slices. Sprinkle with salt and pepper. Top with watercress leaves.
3. Assemble the Sandwiches: Place the remaining bread slices, cream cheese side down, over the fillings. Gently press to adhere.
4. Cut and Serve: Cut each sandwich into triangles or rectangles. Serve immediately or cover with a damp paper towel and plastic wrap to prevent the bread from drying out.

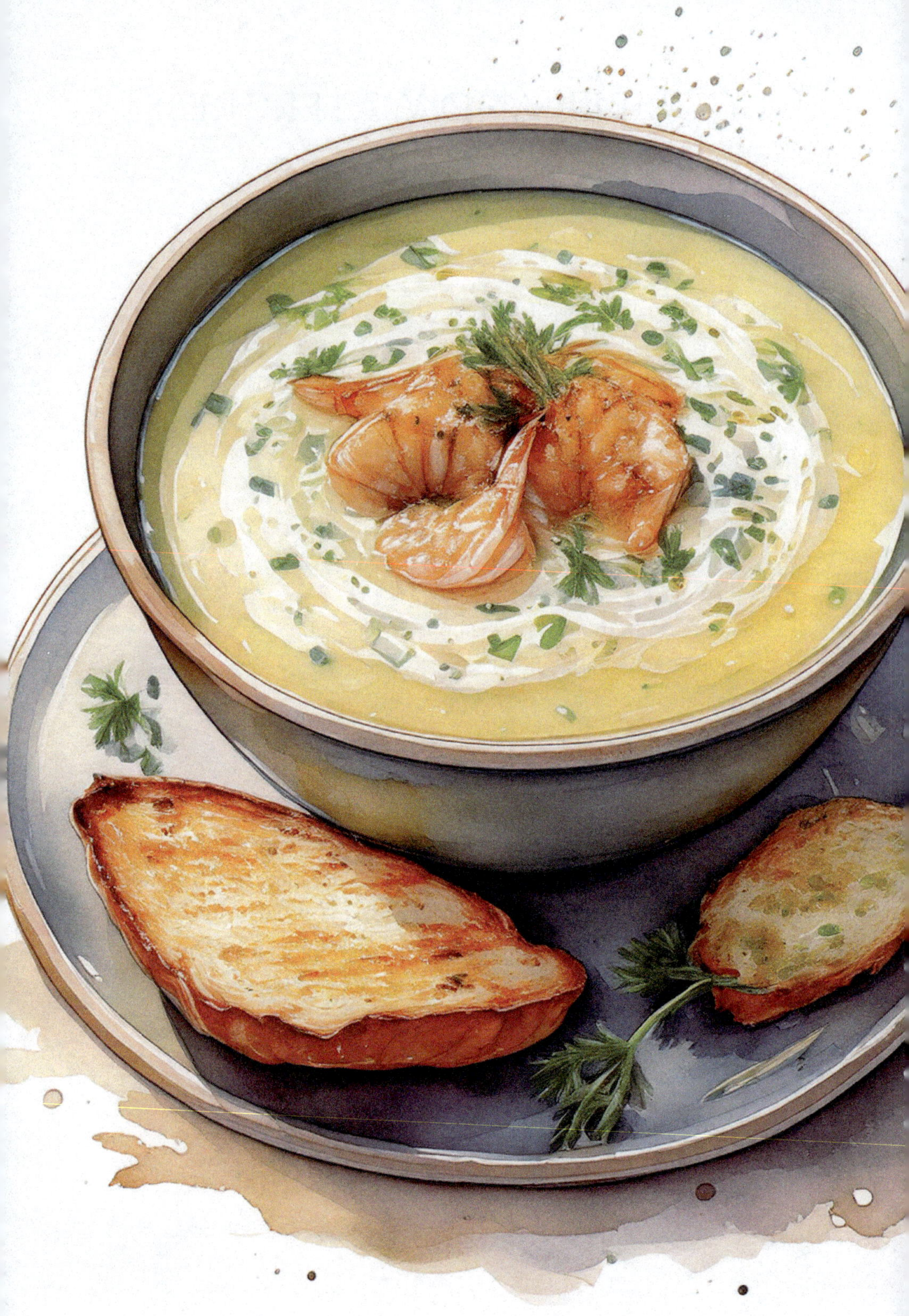

# Creamy New England Clam Chowder

**Ingredients:**

- 4 slices bacon, diced
- 1 medium onion, diced
- 2 stalks celery, diced
- 2 tablespoons all-purpose flour
- 3 cups clam juice
- 1 cup heavy cream
- 1 bay leaf
- 1 pound potatoes, diced
- 2 cans (6.5 ounces each) chopped clams, drained
- Salt and pepper to taste
- Fresh parsley, chopped (for garnish)

**Instructions:**

1. In a large pot or Dutch oven, cook the diced bacon over medium heat until crispy.
2. Remove the cooked bacon from the pot and set aside, leaving the bacon drippings in the pot.
3. Add the diced onion and celery to the pot and cook until softened, about 5 minutes.
4. Stir in the flour and cook for an additional 2 minutes to make a roux.
5. Gradually whisk in the clam juice, making sure to scrape up any browned bits from the bottom of the pot.
6. Add the heavy cream, bay leaf, diced potatoes, and drained clams to the pot. Bring the chowder to a simmer.
7. Simmer the chowder, stirring occasionally, until the potatoes are tender, about 15-20 minutes.
8. Season the chowder with salt and pepper to taste.
9. Ladle the clam chowder into bowls and garnish with the crispy bacon and chopped parsley before serving.

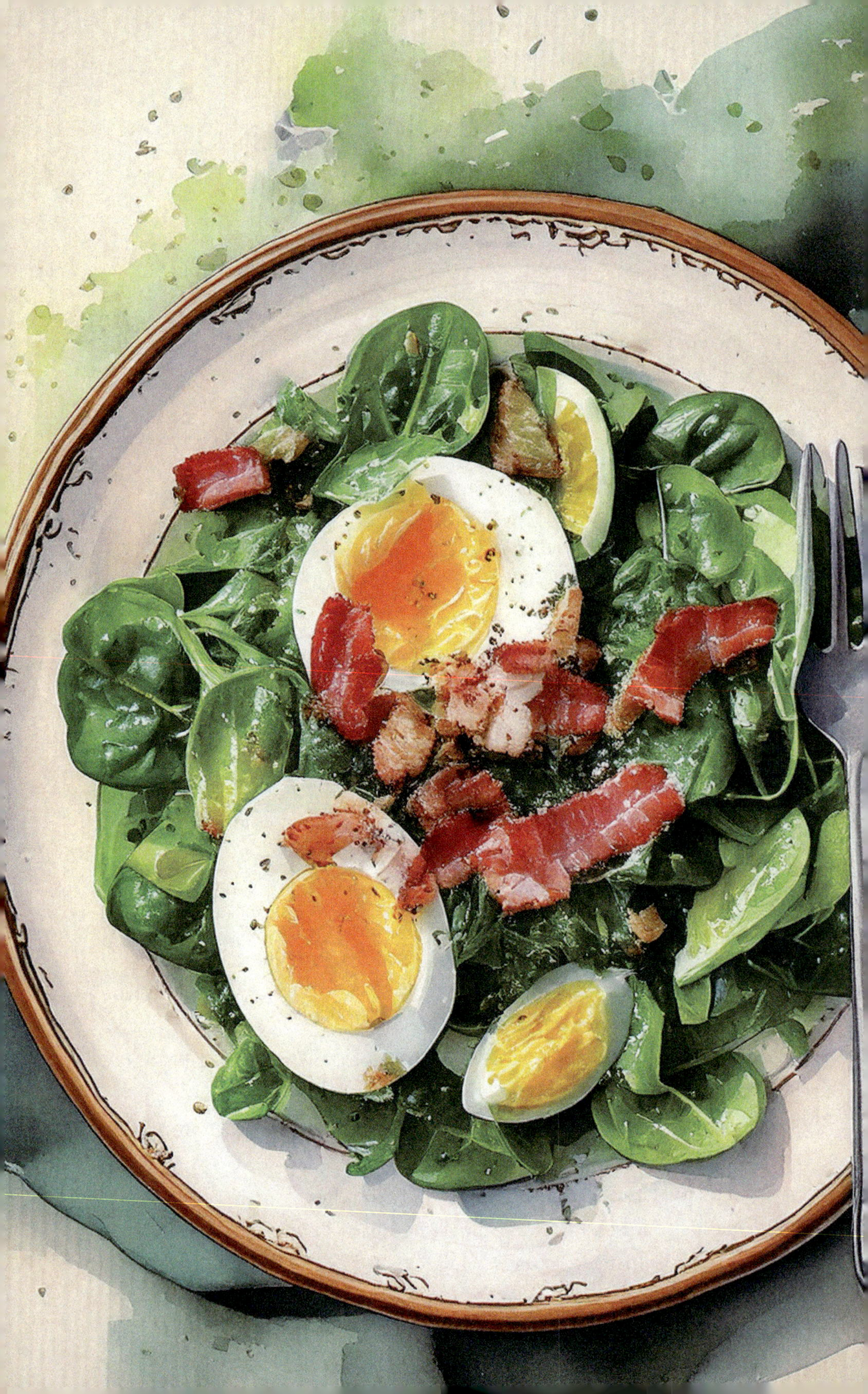

# Spinach and Bacon Salad with Warm Dressing

A fresh and satisfying dish, this salad features warm, tangy bacon dressing—a nod to the resourceful cooking of the era. It's perfect as a light lunch or a side dish.

Ingredients:
- 6 cups fresh spinach leaves, washed and dried
- 4 slices bacon, cooked and crumbled
- 1 small red onion, thinly sliced
- 2 hard-boiled eggs, sliced

For the Dressing:
- 3 tablespoons bacon drippings (reserved from cooking)
- 2 tablespoons red wine vinegar
- 1 tablespoon Dijon mustard
- 1 teaspoon sugar
- Salt and freshly ground black pepper

Instructions:
1. Prepare the Salad Base: Arrange the spinach leaves on a serving platter or individual plates. Top with crumbled bacon, red onion slices, and hard-boiled egg slices.
2. Make the Dressing: In a small saucepan, heat the bacon drippings over medium heat. Whisk in the vinegar, mustard, sugar, salt, and pepper. Cook for 1–2 minutes, until warmed through.
3. Dress the Salad: Drizzle the warm dressing over the salad just before serving. Toss lightly to coat and enjoy immediately.

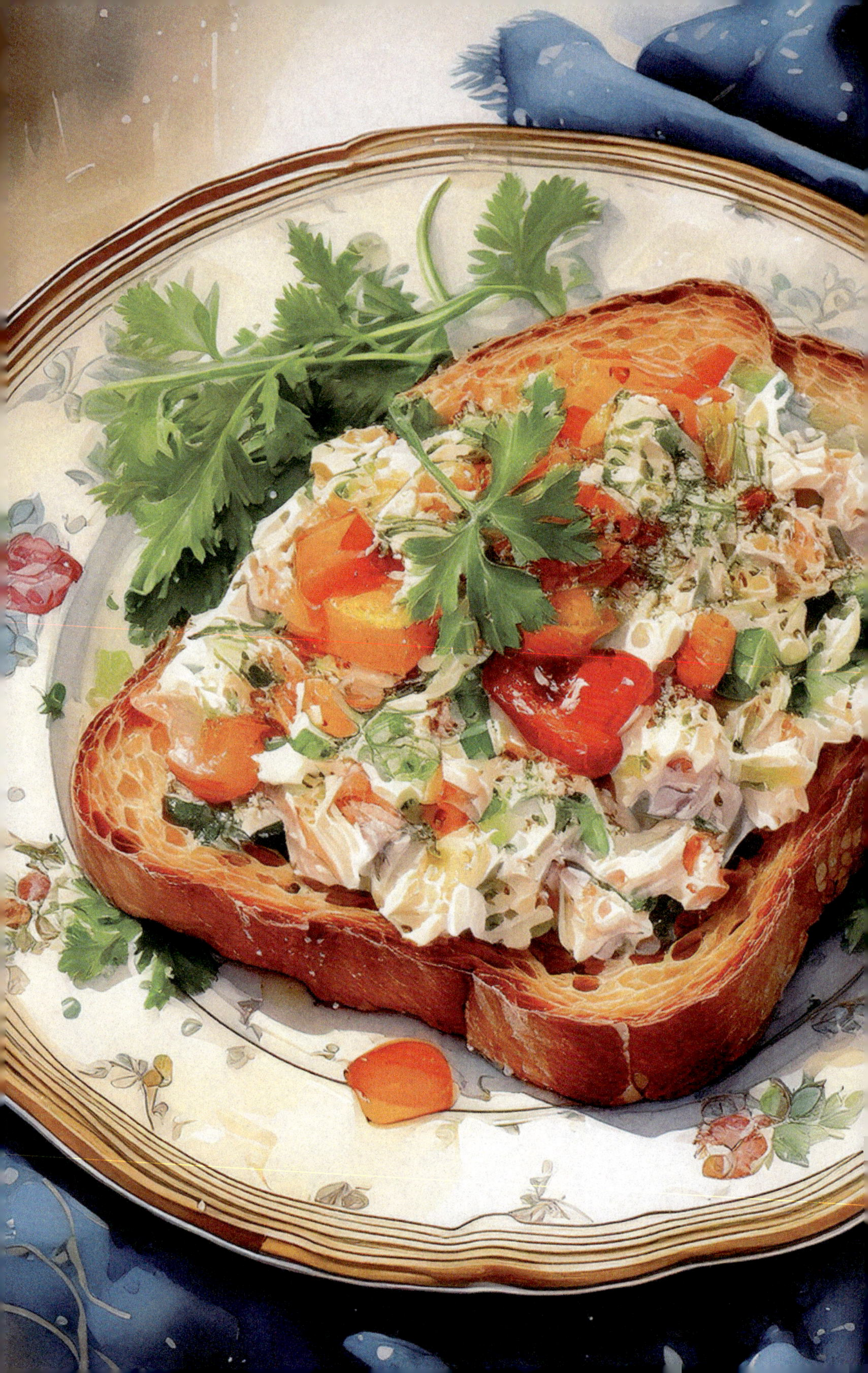

# Victorian Chicken Salad

A dish Meg might have served while hosting one of her "elegant" luncheons. This chicken salad balances simplicity with sophistication, much like Meg herself.

Serves: 4

Ingredients:
- 2 cups cooked chicken, shredded or diced
- 1/2 cup mayonnaise
- 1 teaspoon Dijon mustard
- 1 teaspoon lemon juice
- 1/4 cup celery, finely chopped
- 1/4 cup red grapes, halved
- Salt and freshly ground black pepper, to taste
- Lettuce leaves or bread, for serving

Instructions:
1. Combine Ingredients: In a large bowl, mix the mayonnaise, Dijon mustard, and lemon juice until smooth. Stir in the celery and grapes.
2. Add the Chicken: Fold in the cooked chicken, ensuring it's evenly coated in the dressing. Season with salt and pepper to taste.
3. Serve: Spoon the chicken salad onto lettuce leaves for a light meal or between slices of bread for a sandwich.

Tip: Add a sprinkle of fresh herbs, like parsley or tarragon, for extra flavor.

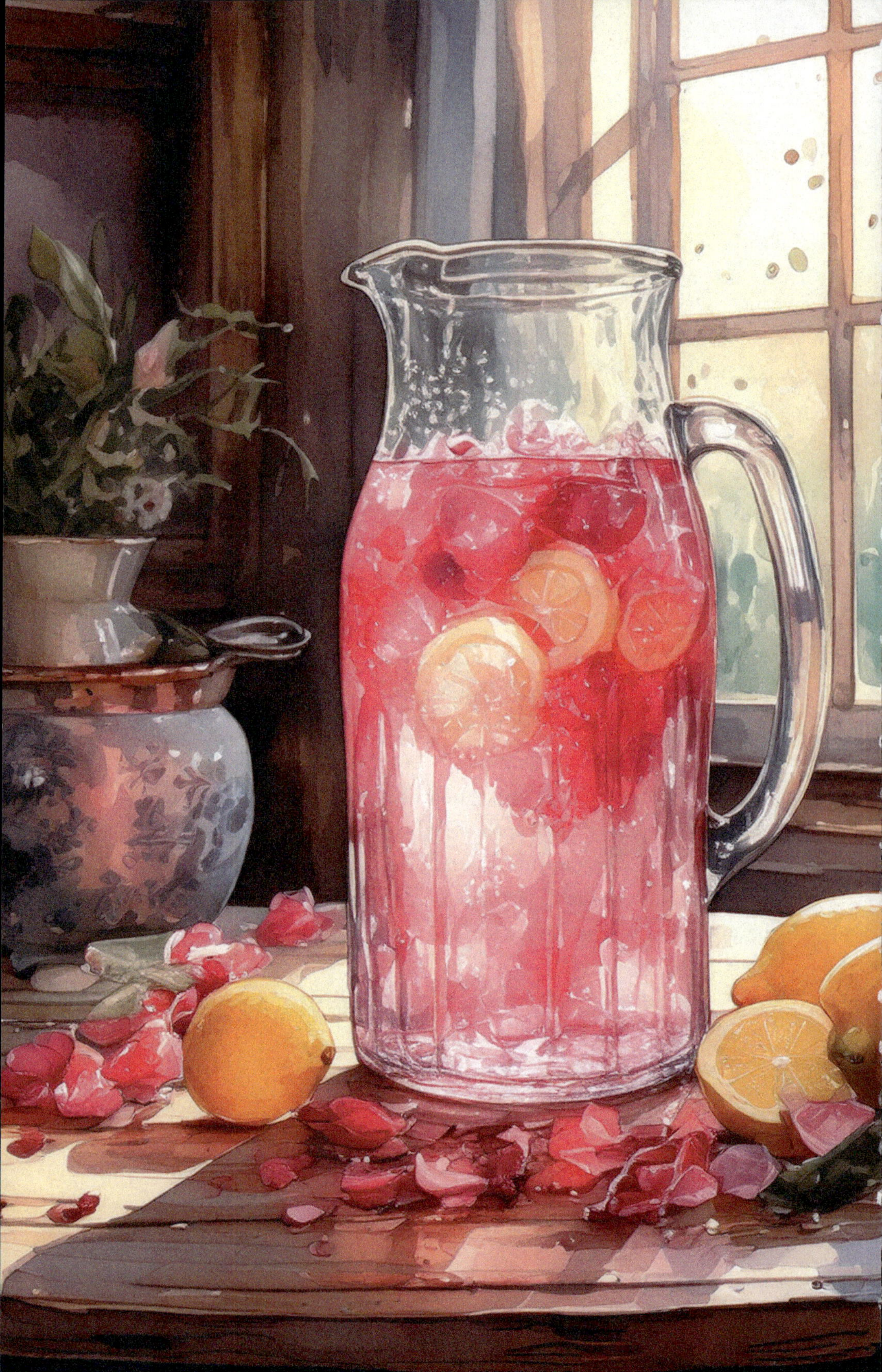

# Rose Petal Lemonade

Serves: 4

Connection to Little Women: Amy's flair for beauty and refinement shines in this elegant lemonade, infused with the subtle fragrance of rose petals. It's a drink that's as delightful to look at as it is to sip.

Ingredients:
- 4 cups water
- 1 cup granulated sugar
- 1/4 cup fresh or dried edible rose petals (plus extra for garnish)
- 1 cup freshly squeezed lemon juice (from about 4–5 lemons)
- Ice, for serving

Instructions:
1. Make the Rose Syrup: In a saucepan, bring the water and sugar to a gentle boil, stirring until the sugar dissolves. Remove from heat and stir in the rose petals. Let steep for 15–20 minutes, then strain and cool.
2. Mix the Lemonade: In a pitcher, combine the rose syrup with the lemon juice. Stir well and adjust sweetness to taste.
3. Serve: Fill glasses with ice and pour the lemonade over. Garnish with a few rose petals.

Tip: Chill the lemonade for at least an hour before serving for the best flavor.

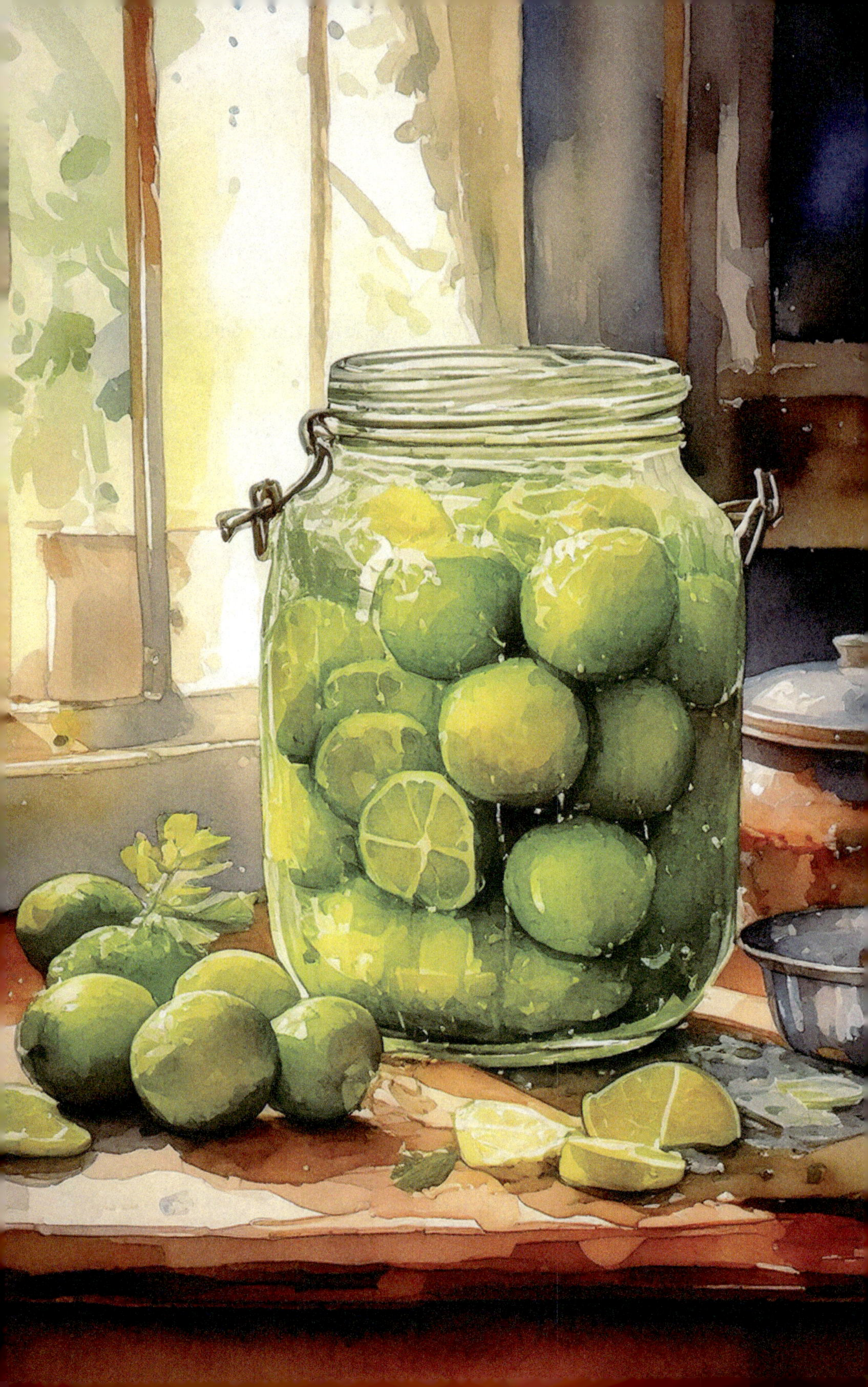

# PICKLED LIMES

Serves: 4 (as a snack or garnish)

Amy's love for pickled limes is legendary, symbolizing childhood indulgence and the trends of the time. Recreate this tangy treat with a simple brine.

Ingredients:
- 6 small limes, washed thoroughly
- 1/4 cup kosher salt
- 1/4 cup sugar
- 2 cups water
- 1/4 cup white vinegar

Instructions:
1. Prepare the Limes: Cut small slits into each lime to allow the brine to penetrate.
2. Make the Brine: In a saucepan, combine the salt, sugar, water, and vinegar. Heat until the salt and sugar dissolve. Cool slightly.
3. Pickle the Limes: Place the limes in a clean jar and pour the brine over them, ensuring they are submerged. Seal tightly.
4. Store: Let sit at room temperature for 1 week, shaking occasionally. Refrigerate after opening.

Tip: Serve as a garnish or enjoy as a tangy snack.

# Chapter 3: Hearty Suppers

The March family often made do with simple yet nourishing meals that warmed their hearts and bodies. These hearty suppers celebrate their New England roots and the comforting flavors that would have graced their table.

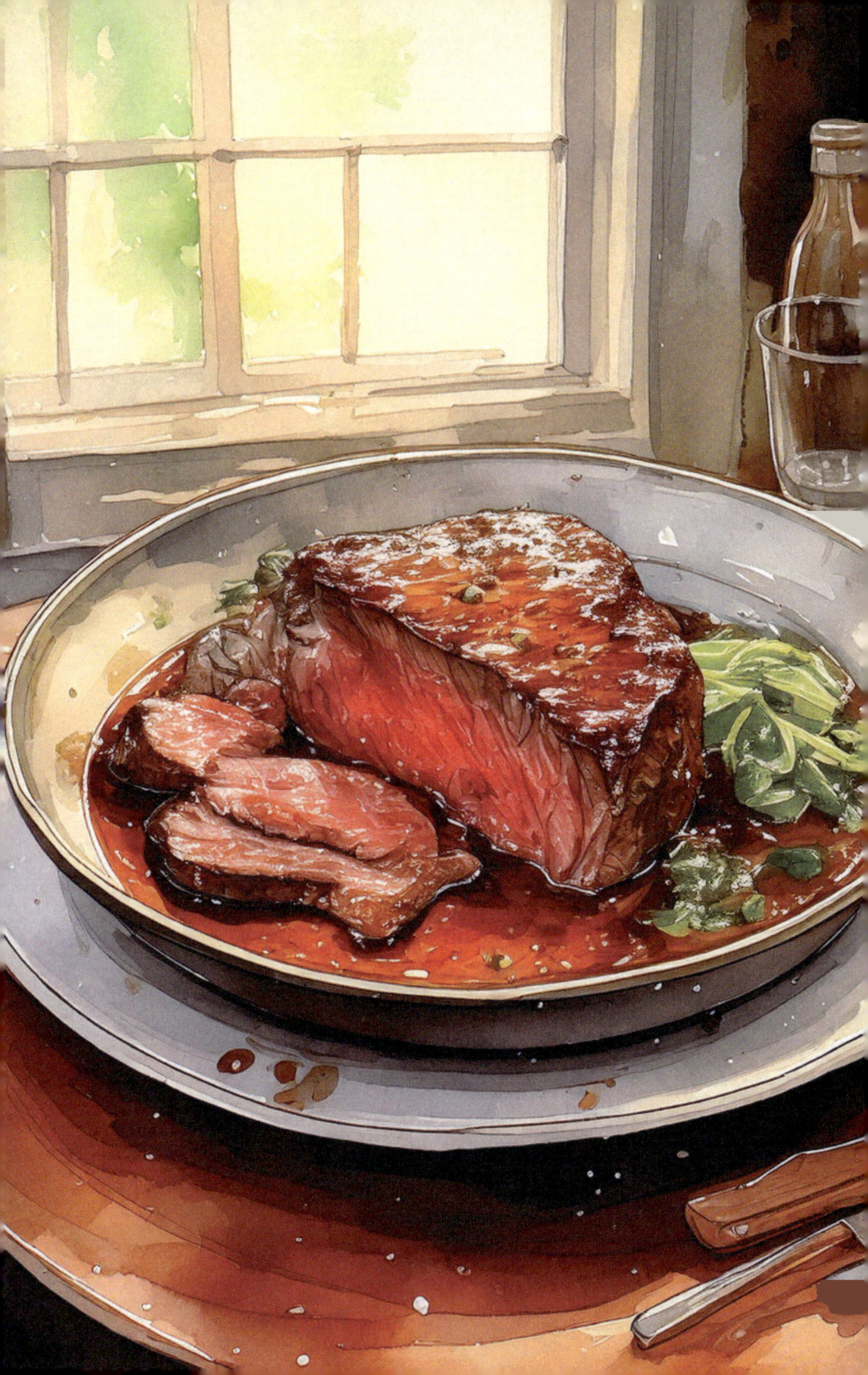

# Mrs. March's Roast Beef with Pan Gravy

A roast beef dinner would have been a special occasion meal for the March family, served during a rare celebration or a gathering with loved ones. Mrs. March's careful and loving preparation shines through in this classic dish.

Serves: 6

Ingredients for the Roast Beef:
- 3-4 pound boneless beef roast (chuck or round)
- 2 teaspoons kosher salt
- 1 teaspoon freshly ground black pepper
- 2 tablespoons olive oil
- 1 medium onion, sliced
- 2 cloves garlic, minced
- 1 cup beef broth
- 1 teaspoon dried thyme
- 1 teaspoon dried rosemary

Ingredients for the Pan Gravy:
- 2 tablespoons all-purpose flour
- 1 cup beef broth or drippings from the roast
- Salt and freshly ground black pepper, to taste

Instructions:

1. Prepare the Roast: Preheat your oven to 325°F (165°C). Rub the roast with salt and pepper.
2. Sear the Roast: Heat olive oil in a large oven-safe skillet or Dutch oven over medium-high heat. Sear the roast on all sides until browned, about 4-5 minutes per side. Remove the roast and set aside.
3. Cook the Aromatics: Add the sliced onion and garlic to the skillet. Cook until softened, about 3 minutes. Add the beef broth, thyme, and rosemary. Return the roast to the skillet.
4. Roast: Cover the skillet with a lid or aluminum foil and roast in the oven for 2.5-3 hours, or until the roast is tender.
5. Make the Gravy: Once the roast is done, remove it from the skillet and set aside to rest. Strain the drippings, reserving about 1 cup. In the same skillet, whisk the flour into the drippings over medium heat. Gradually add the reserved drippings or beef broth, whisking constantly until thickened. Season with salt and pepper.
6. Serve: Slice the roast and drizzle with pan gravy.

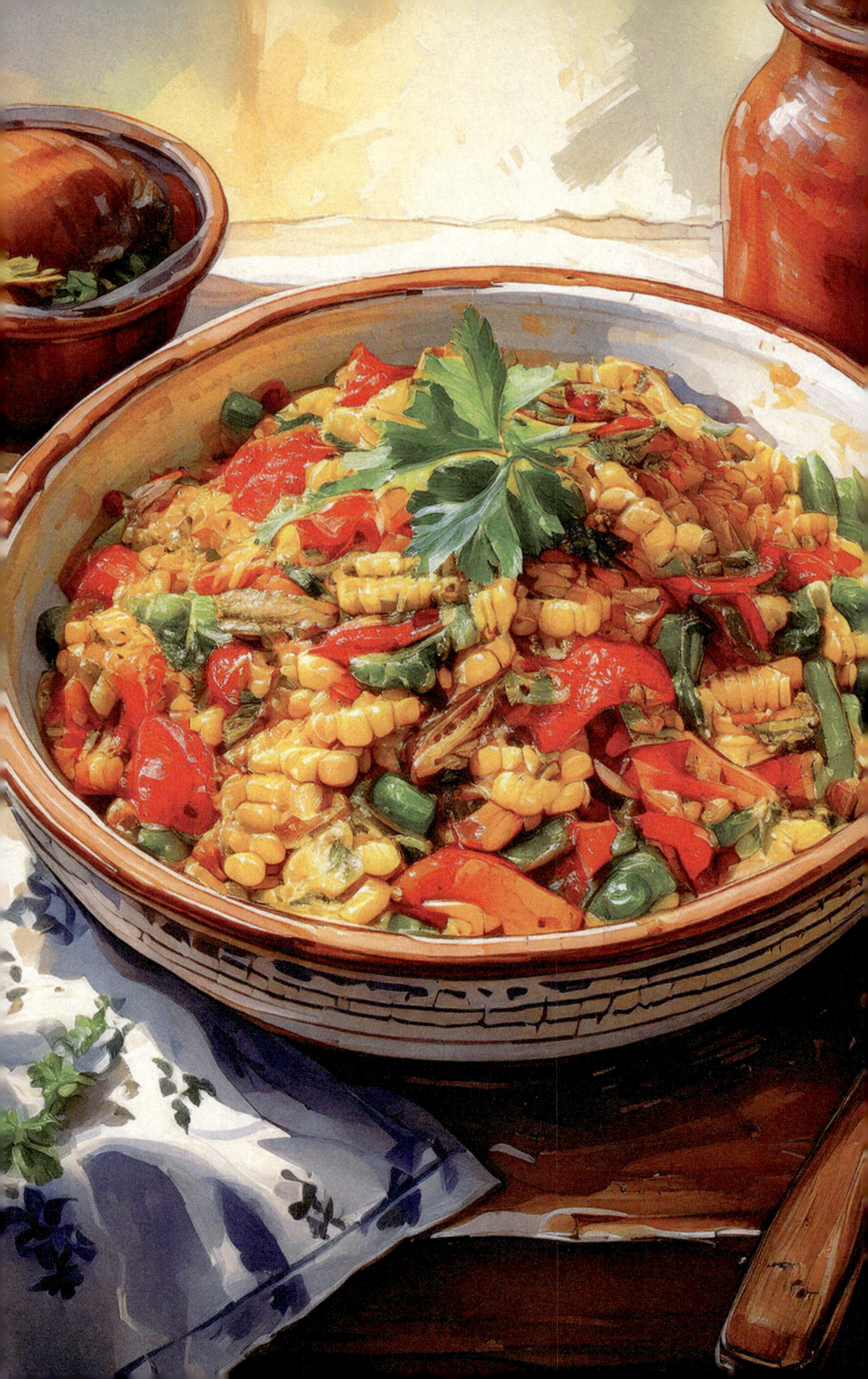

# Succotash: A Classic New England Side

This classic New England dish of corn and beans embodies the frugality and resourcefulness of the March family's meals. It's a side dish full of history and flavor.

Serves: 4

Ingredients:
- 2 cups fresh or frozen corn kernels
- 1 cup shelled lima beans (fresh or frozen)
- 2 tablespoons unsalted butter
- 1 small onion, diced
- 1 red bell pepper, diced
- 1 teaspoon dried thyme
- Salt and freshly ground black pepper, to taste
- Fresh parsley, chopped, for garnish

Instructions:
1. Prepare the Vegetables: Bring a pot of salted water to a boil. Cook the lima beans for 5 minutes, then add the corn and cook for another 2 minutes. Drain and set aside.
2. Sauté Aromatics: In a large skillet, melt the butter over medium heat. Add the onion and red bell pepper. Cook until softened, about 5 minutes.
3. Combine Ingredients: Stir in the corn, lima beans, and thyme. Cook for 3-4 minutes, stirring occasionally. Season with salt and pepper.
4. Serve: Transfer to a serving dish and garnish with fresh parsley.

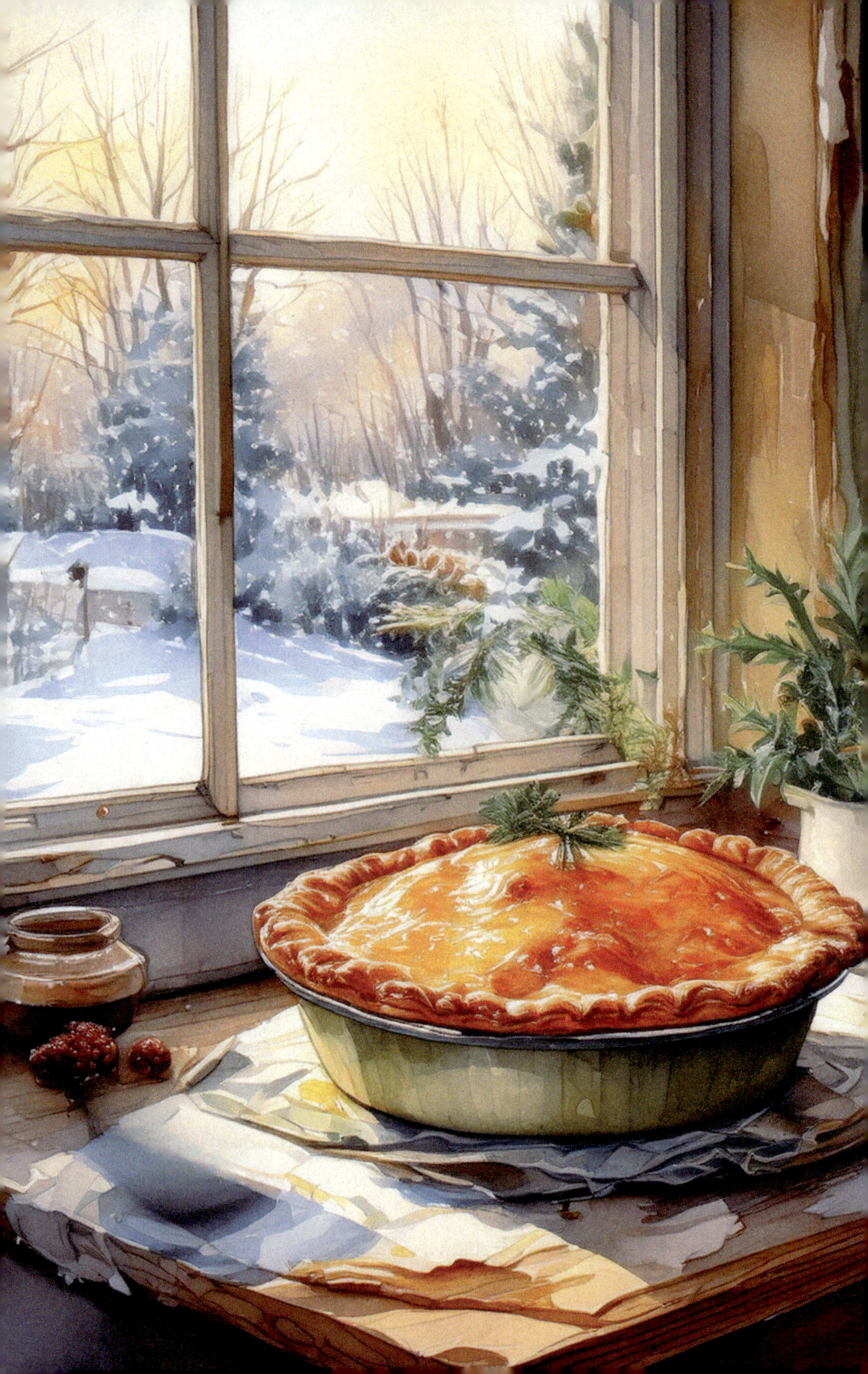

# Colonial Chicken Pot Pie

A hearty chicken pot pie would have been a comforting, one-dish meal, perfect for a cold New England evening. Its rustic, flaky crust and creamy filling represent the resourcefulness of the March family.

Serves: 6

Ingredients for the Filling:
- 1/4 cup unsalted butter
- 1/4 cup all-purpose flour
- 2 cups chicken broth
- 1 cup whole milk
- 2 cups cooked chicken, shredded
- 1 cup diced carrots
- 1 cup diced celery
- 1 cup peas (fresh or frozen)
- 1 teaspoon dried thyme
- Salt and freshly ground black pepper, to taste

Ingredients for the Crust:
- 1 sheet puff pastry, thawed
- 1 large egg, beaten (for egg wash)

Instructions:

1. Prepare the Filling: Melt butter in a large skillet over medium heat. Stir in the flour and cook for 1-2 minutes to form a roux. Gradually whisk in the chicken broth and milk until smooth. Simmer until thickened, about 5 minutes. Stir in the chicken, carrots, celery, peas, thyme, salt, and pepper. Cook for another 5 minutes. Remove from heat.
2. Assemble the Pie: Preheat your oven to 375°F (190°C). Pour the filling into a deep-dish pie pan or casserole dish. Place the puff pastry over the filling, trimming any excess. Seal the edges and cut small slits in the center for ventilation. Brush with egg wash.
3. Bake: Bake for 30-35 minutes, or until the crust is golden brown and puffed.
4. Serve: Let cool for 5 minutes before serving.

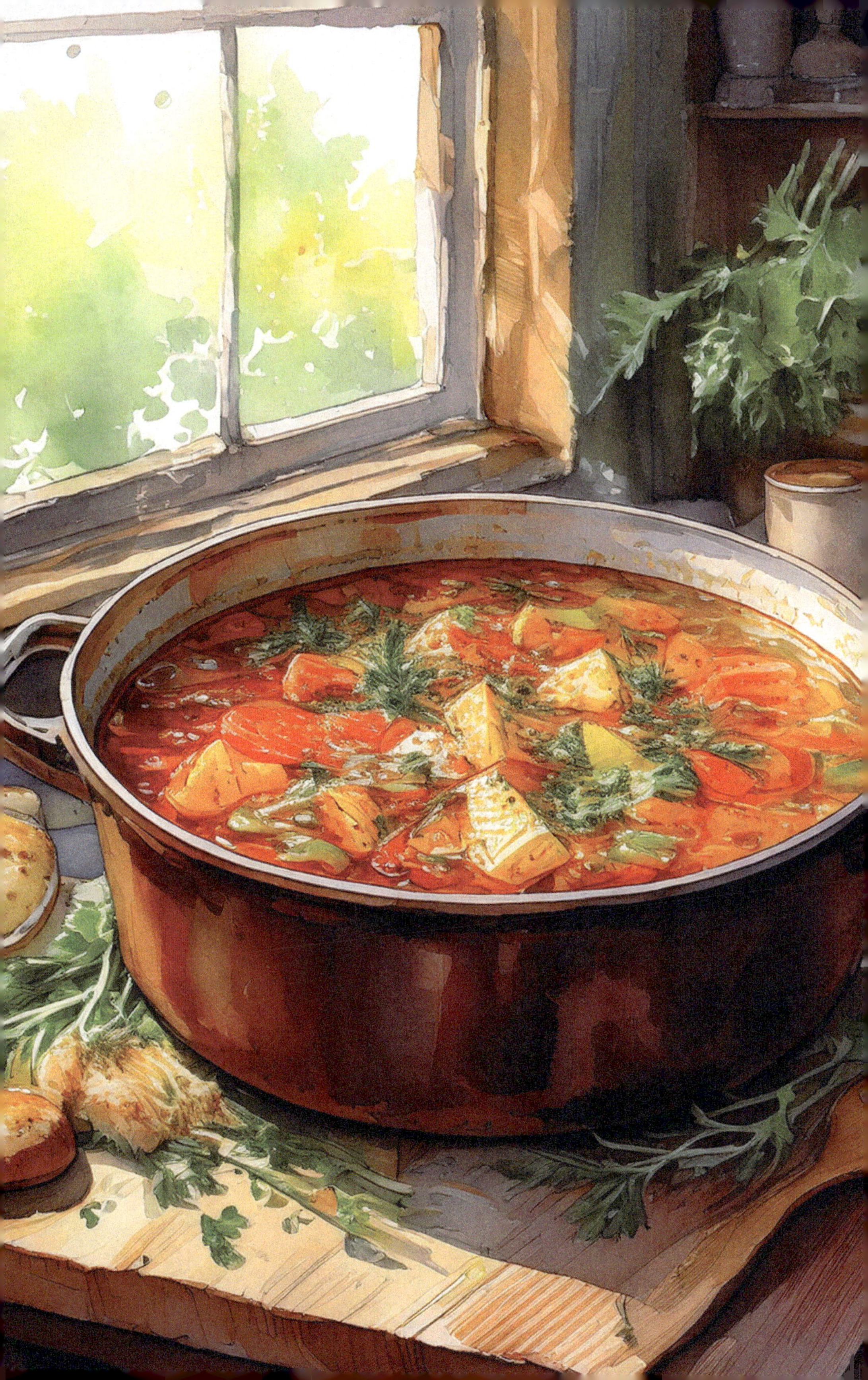

# Jo's Rustic Vegetable Stew

Connection to Little Women: Jo's practicality and love for simple, hearty meals inspired this vegetable stew, which uses seasonal ingredients to create a nourishing dish.

Serves: 6

Ingredients:
- 2 tablespoons olive oil
- 1 medium onion, diced
- 2 garlic cloves, minced
- 2 carrots, sliced
- 2 celery stalks, diced
- 2 medium potatoes, cubed
- 1 cup diced tomatoes (fresh or canned)
- 4 cups vegetable broth
- 1 teaspoon dried thyme
- 1 teaspoon dried rosemary
- 1 cup green beans, trimmed and halved
- Salt and freshly ground black pepper, to taste
- Fresh parsley, chopped (for garnish)

Instructions:

1. Sauté Aromatics: Heat olive oil in a large pot over medium heat. Add the onion and garlic and cook until fragrant, about 3 minutes.
2. Add Vegetables: Stir in the carrots, celery, potatoes, and tomatoes. Cook for 5 minutes.
3. Simmer the Stew: Add the vegetable broth, thyme, and rosemary. Bring to a boil, then reduce the heat and simmer for 20-25 minutes, or until the vegetables are tender.
4. Add Green Beans: Stir in the green beans and cook for another 5-7 minutes. Season with salt and pepper to taste.
5. Serve: Ladle into bowls and garnish with fresh parsley.

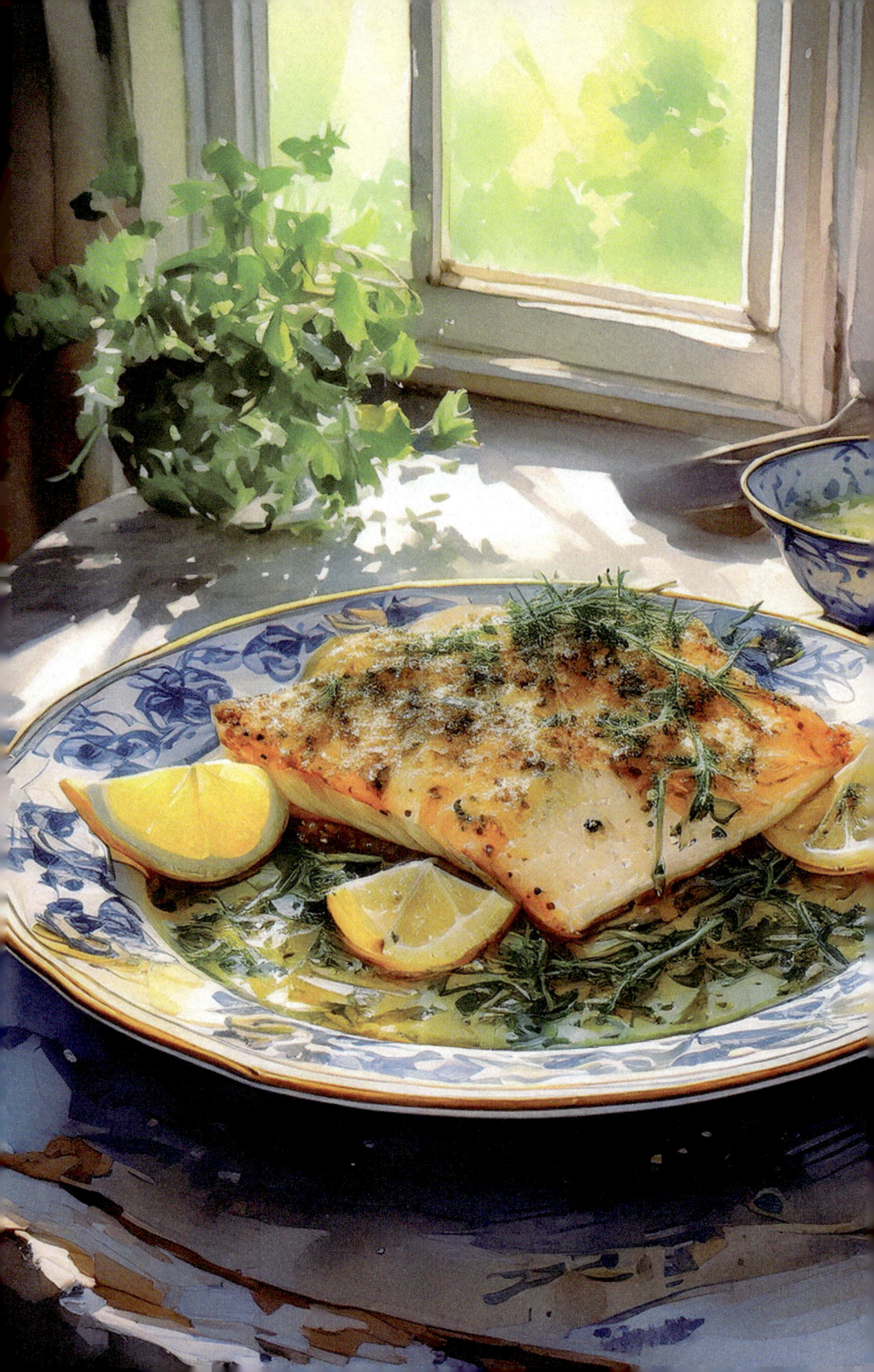

# Baked Fish with Herbs and Lemon

This simple yet flavorful dish reflects the March family's resourceful use of fresh ingredients, celebrating the light and wholesome flavors of New England's coastal influence.

Serves: 4

Ingredients:
- 4 fillets of white fish (such as cod, haddock, or flounder)
- 2 tablespoons olive oil
- 2 cloves garlic, minced
- 1 lemon, thinly sliced (plus juice of 1/2 lemon)
- 2 tablespoons fresh parsley, chopped
- 1 tablespoon fresh dill, chopped (optional)
- Salt and freshly ground black pepper, to taste

Instructions:
1. Preheat the Oven: Preheat the oven to 375°F (190°C). Line a baking dish with parchment paper or lightly grease it with olive oil.
2. Prepare the Fish: Place the fish fillets in the baking dish. Drizzle with olive oil and lemon juice, and season with salt and pepper.
3. Add Garlic and Herbs: Sprinkle the minced garlic, parsley, and dill over the fish. Arrange lemon slices on top of and around the fillets.
4. Bake: Cover the dish with aluminum foil and bake for 15-20 minutes, depending on the thickness of the fillets, until the fish is opaque and flakes easily with a fork.
5. Serve: Carefully transfer the fish to plates, spooning some of the pan juices over the fillets. Garnish with additional parsley if desired.

Tip: Serve alongside Succotash or Buttery Mashed Turnips and Potatoes for a well-rounded meal.

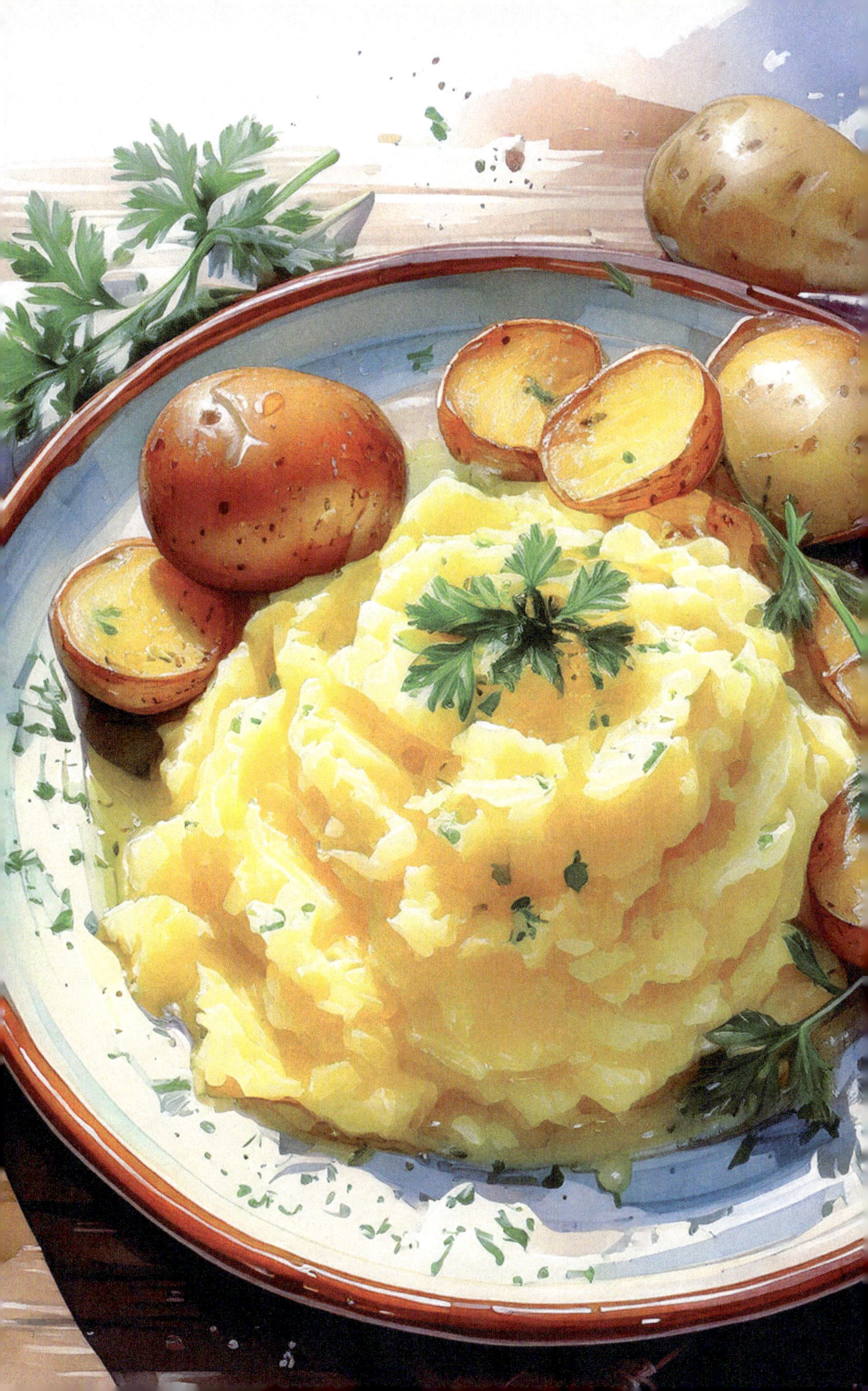

# Buttery Mashed Turnips and Potatoes

This dish, combining hearty potatoes and earthy turnips, represents the practicality of the March family's meals. It's both humble and satisfying, a true New England comfort food.

Serves: 6

Ingredients:
- 1.5 pounds Yukon Gold potatoes, peeled and cubed
- 1.5 pounds turnips, peeled and cubed
- 1/4 cup unsalted butter
- 1/2 cup whole milk (or more, as needed)
- 1 teaspoon salt
- 1/2 teaspoon freshly ground black pepper
- 1 tablespoon fresh chives, chopped (optional, for garnish)

Instructions:
1. Cook the Vegetables: Bring a large pot of salted water to a boil. Add the potatoes and turnips and cook for 15-20 minutes, or until fork-tender. Drain well.
2. Mash the Vegetables: Return the potatoes and turnips to the pot. Add the butter, milk, salt, and pepper. Use a potato masher or hand mixer to mash until smooth. Adjust the milk as needed to reach your desired consistency.
3. Taste and Adjust: Season with additional salt and pepper if needed.
4. Serve: Transfer to a serving bowl and garnish with chopped chives if desired.

Tip: These mashed turnips and potatoes pair wonderfully with Mrs. March's Roast Beef with Pan Gravy for a hearty, comforting supper.

# Chapter 4: Sweet Treats and Desserts

Desserts in Little Women are more than just indulgences—they are moments of joy, expressions of care, and sometimes, a means of lifting spirits in difficult times. Whether it's Meg's attempt to impress with her molasses cookies, or a simple apple dessert shared by the family, these sweet treats bring warmth and connection to the March household. This chapter celebrates the enduring charm of Victorian desserts.

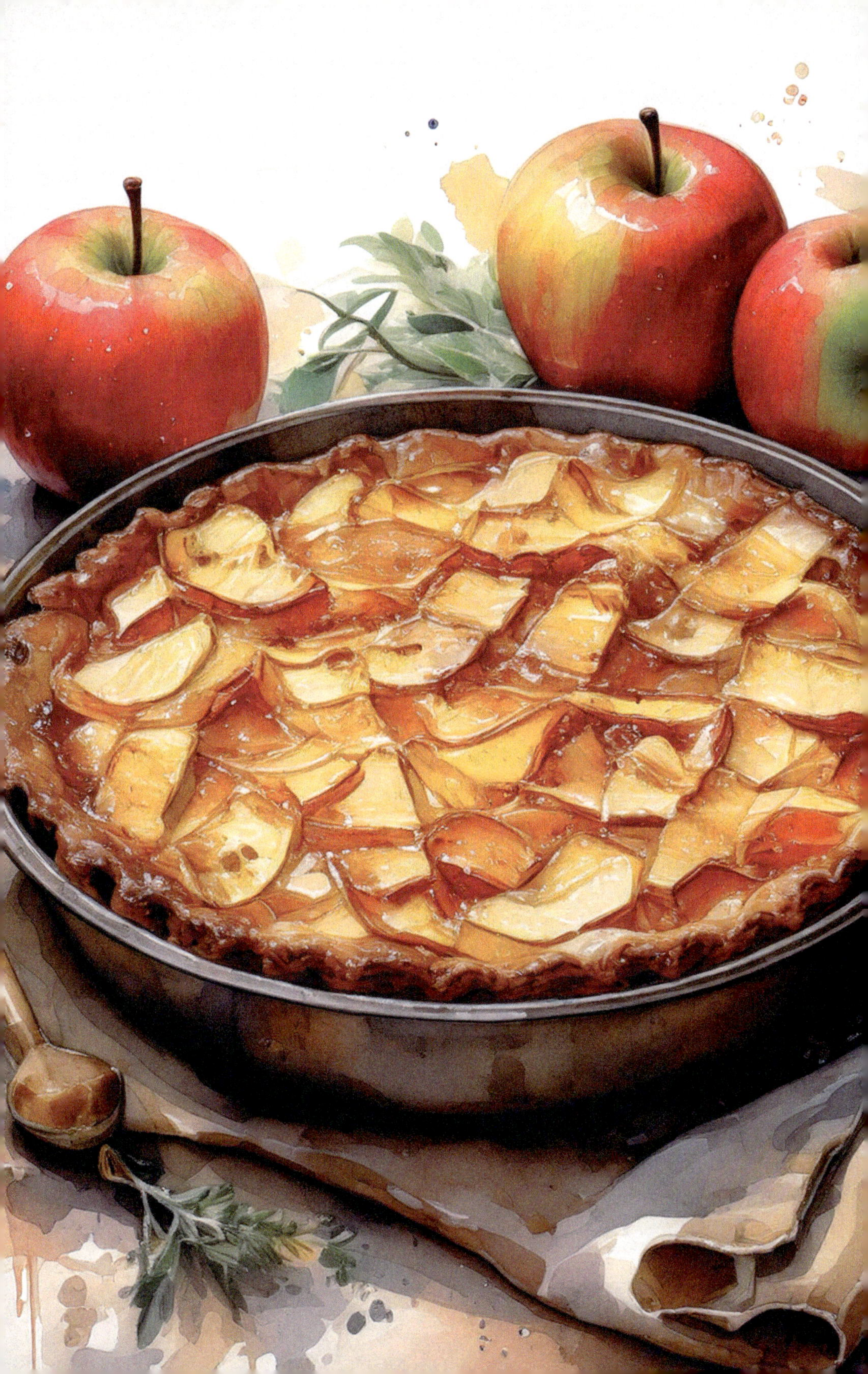

# Apple Pandowdy

This rustic apple dessert is a New England favorite, reflecting the resourceful use of local fruits in the March family's kitchen. The simplicity of this dish aligns perfectly with their humble, heartfelt meals.

Serves: 6-8

Ingredients:
- 6 cups peeled, cored, and sliced apples (Granny Smith or Honeycrisp)
- 1/2 cup brown sugar
- 1 teaspoon ground cinnamon
- 1/4 teaspoon ground nutmeg
- 1/4 teaspoon ground cloves
- 2 tablespoons all-purpose flour
- 1 tablespoon lemon juice
- 1/2 cup unsalted butter, melted
- 1 sheet puff pastry, thawed
- 1 tablespoon milk (for brushing)
- 1 tablespoon granulated sugar (for sprinkling)

Instructions:
1. Preheat the Oven: Preheat your oven to 375°F (190°C). Grease a deep-dish pie pan or 9x9-inch baking dish.
2. Prepare the Apple Filling: In a large bowl, toss the apple slices with brown sugar, cinnamon, nutmeg, cloves, flour, and lemon juice. Transfer the mixture to the prepared dish.
3. Top with Puff Pastry: Lay the puff pastry sheet over the apples, trimming any excess. Tuck the edges into the dish and cut a few small slits in the center for steam to escape.
4. Brush and Sprinkle: Brush the pastry with milk and sprinkle with granulated sugar for a golden, crisp finish.
5. Bake: Bake for 35-40 minutes, or until the pastry is puffed and golden, and the apples are tender and bubbling.
6. Serve: Let cool slightly before serving warm, optionally with a scoop of vanilla ice cream.

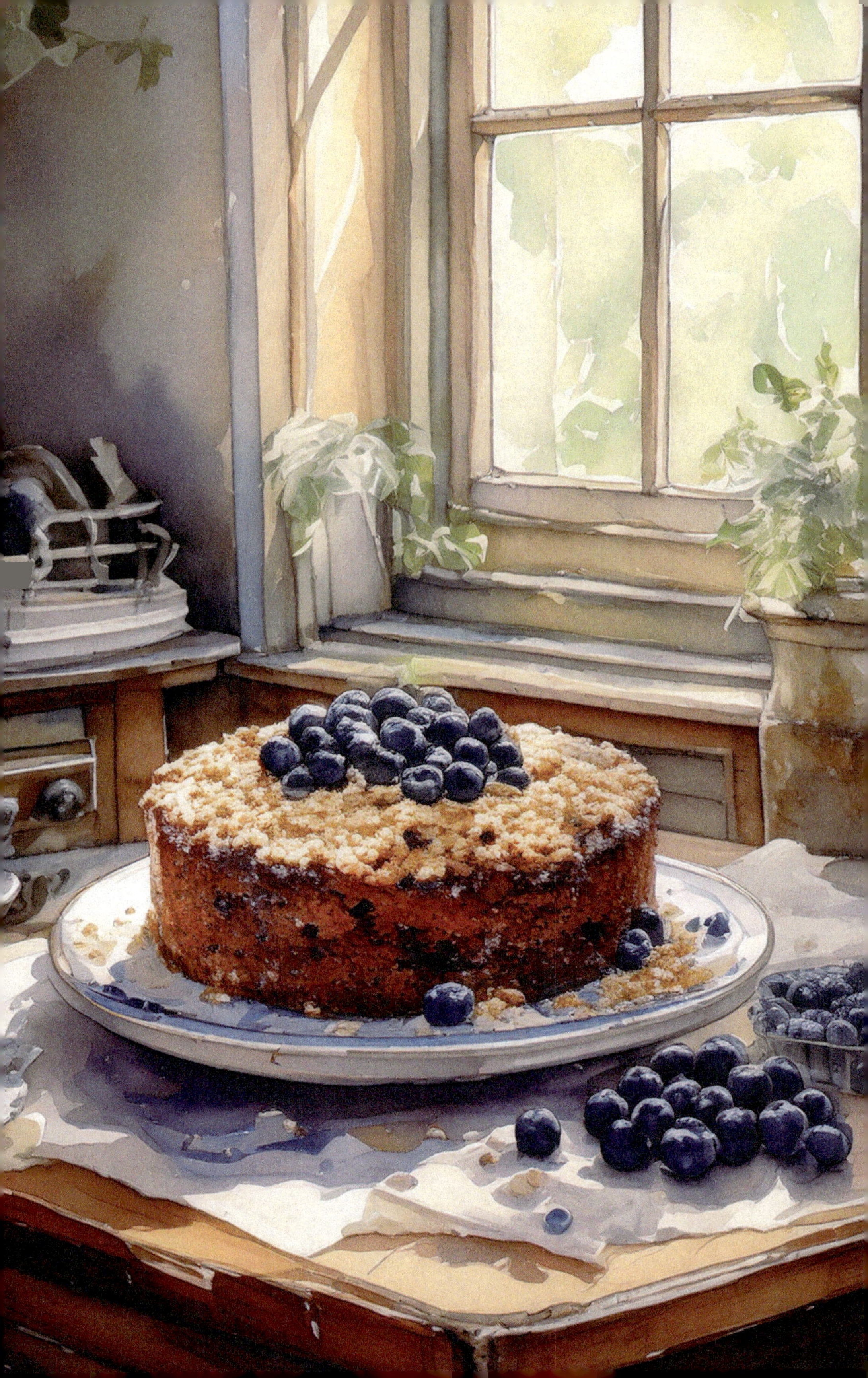

# Blueberry Buckle with Crumb Topping

Blueberries, abundant in New England, were often preserved or baked into desserts like this one. A buckle is the perfect balance between cake and crumble, making it a charming addition to the March family table.

Serves: 6-8

Ingredients for the Cake:
- 2 cups all-purpose flour
- 2 teaspoons baking powder
- 1/2 teaspoon salt
- 1/2 cup unsalted butter, softened
- 3/4 cup granulated sugar
- 1 large egg
- 1 teaspoon vanilla extract
- 1/2 cup whole milk
- 2 cups fresh or frozen blueberries

Ingredients for the Crumb Topping:
- 1/2 cup granulated sugar
- 1/3 cup all-purpose flour
- 1/4 cup unsalted butter, cold and cubed
- 1/2 teaspoon ground cinnamon

Instructions:
1. Preheat the Oven: Preheat the oven to 375°F (190°C). Grease an 8-inch square baking pan.
2. Prepare the Batter: In a medium bowl, whisk together the flour, baking powder, and salt. In a large bowl, cream the butter and sugar until light and fluffy. Beat in the egg and vanilla. Gradually add the dry ingredients, alternating with the milk. Fold in the blueberries.
3. Make the Topping: In a small bowl, mix the sugar, flour, butter, and cinnamon with a pastry cutter or your fingers until crumbly.
4. Assemble and Bake: Spread the batter evenly into the prepared pan. Sprinkle the crumb topping over the batter. Bake for 35-40 minutes, or until a toothpick inserted into the center comes out clean.
5. Serve: Let cool slightly before slicing. Serve warm or at room temperature.

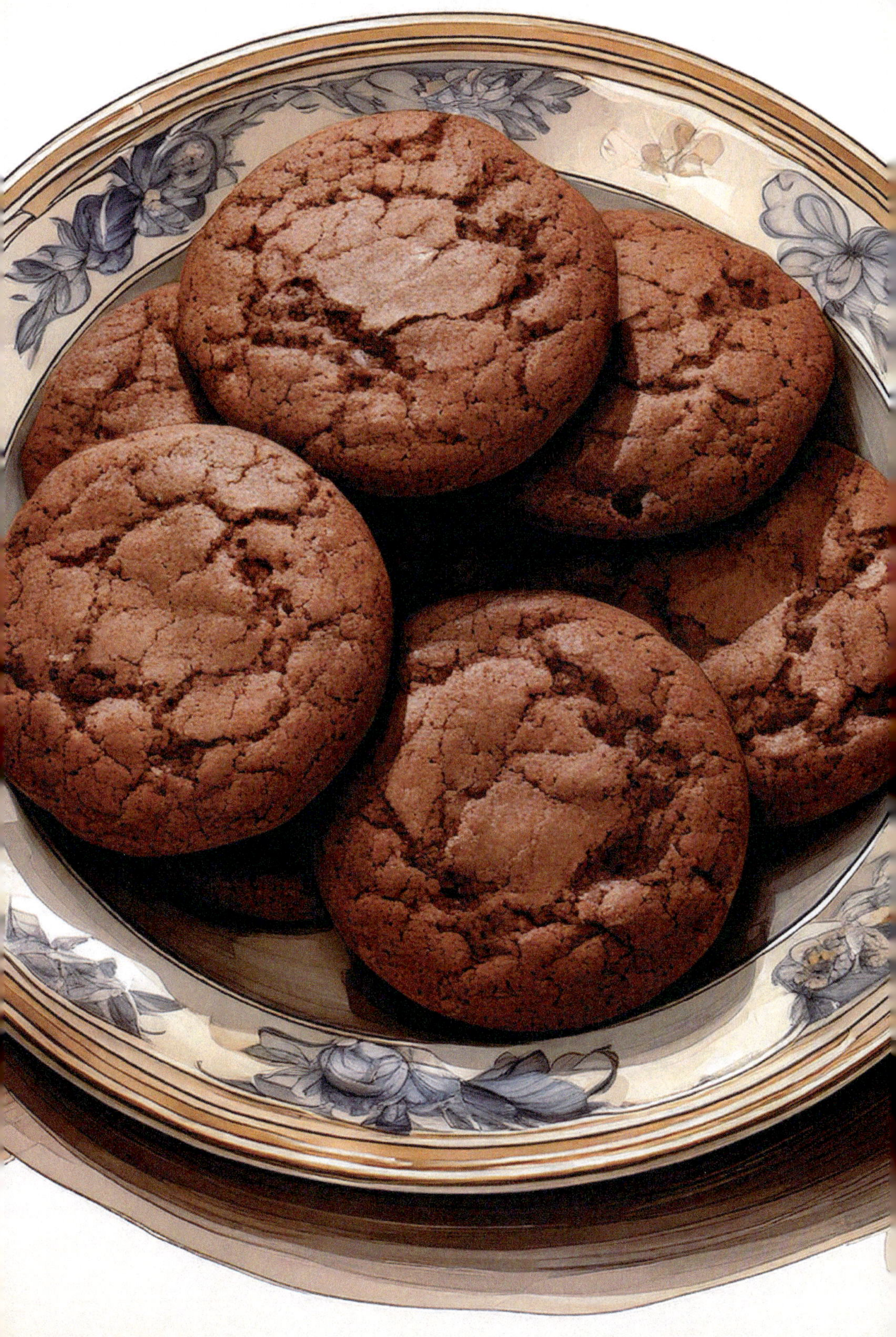

# Meg's Molasses Cookies

Meg's molasses cookies embody her nurturing spirit and love for tradition. These cookies are soft, spiced, and perfect for sharing with family or guests.

Serves: 24 cookies

Ingredients:
- 3/4 cup unsalted butter, softened
- 1 cup brown sugar, packed
- 1/4 cup molasses
- 1 large egg
- 2 1/4 cups all-purpose flour
- 2 teaspoons baking soda
- 1 teaspoon ground cinnamon
- 1 teaspoon ground ginger
- 1/2 teaspoon ground cloves
- 1/4 teaspoon salt
- Additional sugar, for rolling

Instructions:
1. Preheat the Oven: Preheat your oven to 350°F (175°C). Line two baking sheets with parchment paper.
2. Mix the Wet Ingredients: In a large bowl, cream together the butter and brown sugar until light and fluffy. Beat in the molasses and egg until smooth.
3. Combine Dry Ingredients: In a separate bowl, whisk together the flour, baking soda, cinnamon, ginger, cloves, and salt. Gradually add the dry ingredients to the wet mixture, mixing until combined.
4. Shape the Cookies: Roll the dough into 1-inch balls and roll each ball in sugar. Place the cookies 2 inches apart on the prepared baking sheets.
5. Bake: Bake for 8-10 minutes, or until the edges are set but the centers are soft. Let cool on the baking sheet for 2 minutes before transferring to a wire rack.
6. Serve: Enjoy with a glass of milk or a hot cup of tea.

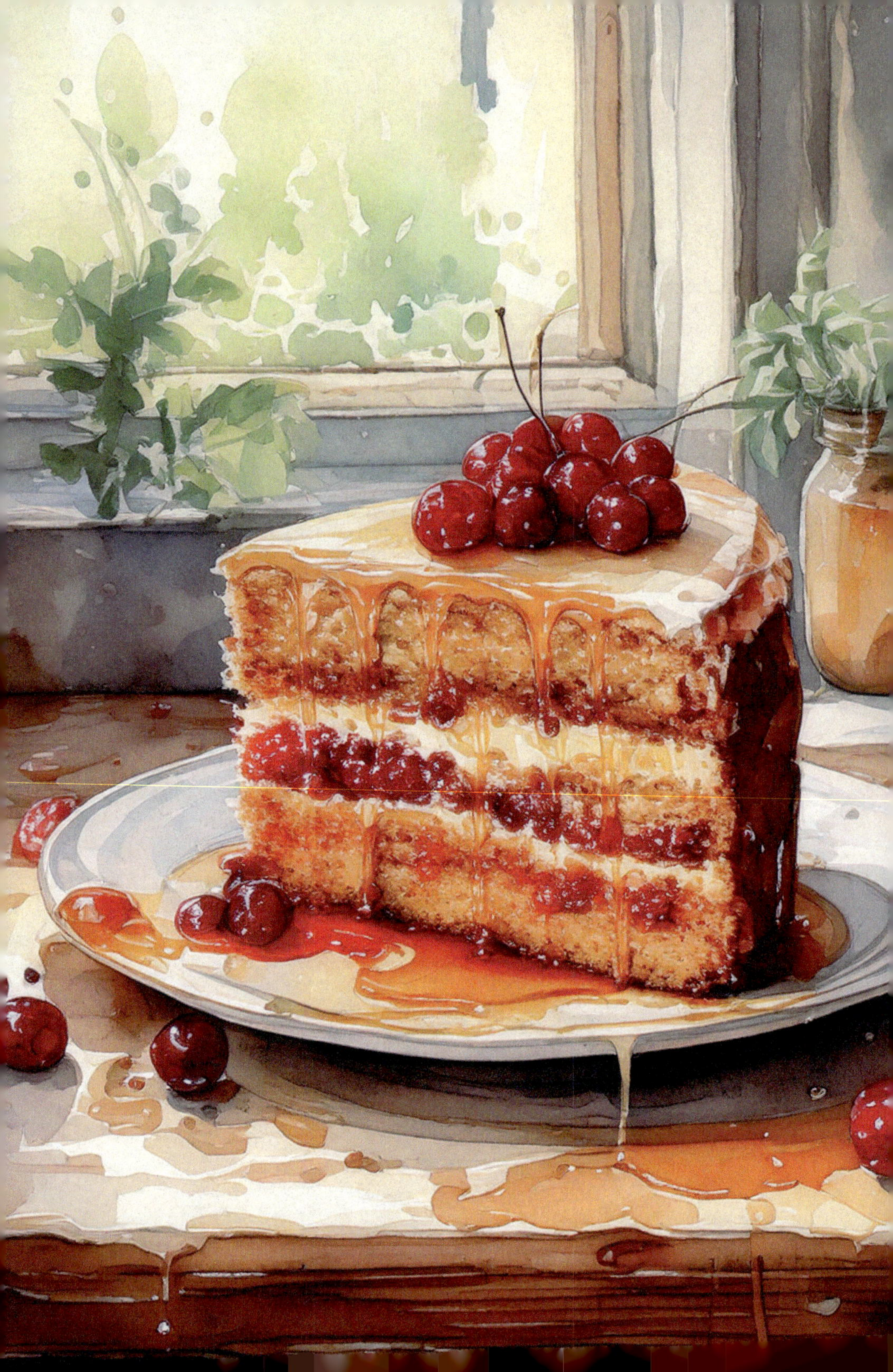

# Cranberry Cake with Warm Vanilla Sauce

Connection to Little Women: Cranberries were widely used in 19th-century New England, and this moist cake would have been a delightful treat for the March family, perfect for gatherings or cozy evenings at home.

Serves: 8

Ingredients for the Cake:
- 2 cups fresh or frozen cranberries
- 1/2 cup granulated sugar (for coating cranberries)
- 2 cups all-purpose flour
- 1 1/2 teaspoons baking powder
- 1/4 teaspoon salt
- 1/2 cup unsalted butter, softened
- 1 cup granulated sugar
- 2 large eggs
- 1 teaspoon vanilla extract
- 1/2 cup whole milk

Ingredients for the Warm Vanilla Sauce:
- 1/2 cup unsalted butter
- 1/2 cup granulated sugar
- 1/2 cup heavy cream
- 1 teaspoon vanilla extract

Instructions:

1. Prepare the Cranberries: Toss the cranberries with 1/2 cup sugar and set aside to macerate for 15 minutes. Preheat the oven to 350°F (175°C) and grease a 9-inch round cake pan.
2. Make the Cake Batter: In a medium bowl, whisk together the flour, baking powder, and salt. In a large bowl, cream the butter and sugar until light and fluffy. Beat in the eggs one at a time, then add the vanilla. Gradually add the dry ingredients, alternating with the milk, until just combined.
3. Assemble and Bake: Fold the cranberries into the batter and pour into the prepared cake pan. Smooth the top and bake for 35–40 minutes, or until a toothpick inserted into the center comes out clean. Cool slightly before serving.
4. Prepare the Vanilla Sauce: In a small saucepan, melt the butter over medium heat. Stir in the sugar and heavy cream. Cook, stirring constantly, for 2–3 minutes, until the sugar dissolves and the sauce thickens slightly. Remove from heat and stir in the vanilla extract.
5. Serve: Slice the warm cake and drizzle with the vanilla sauce. Garnish with additional cranberries, if desired.

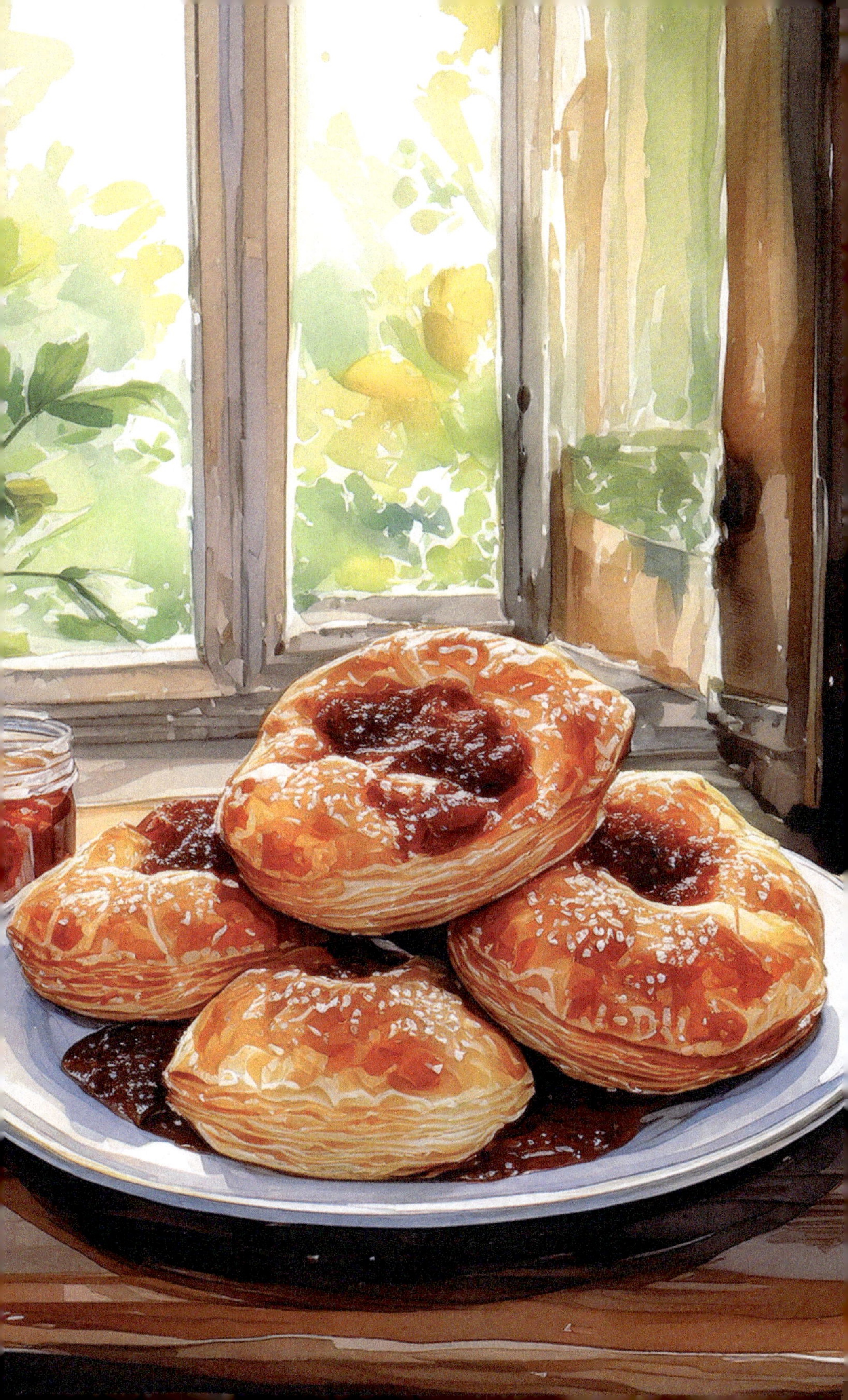

# Concord Grape Jam Tarts

Concord grapes, named after Louisa May Alcott's hometown, make these delightful tarts a tribute to her roots. These charming pastries would have been a treat for the March sisters during tea time or a special gathering.

Serves: 8 tarts

Ingredients:
- 1 sheet puff pastry, thawed
- 1/2 cup Concord grape jam or jelly
- 1 large egg, beaten (for egg wash)
- 1 tablespoon granulated sugar (for sprinkling)

Instructions:

1. Preheat the Oven: Preheat your oven to 375°F (190°C). Line a baking sheet with parchment paper.
2. Cut the Pastry: Roll out the puff pastry on a lightly floured surface. Cut into 8 equal rectangles or circles using a knife or pastry cutter.
3. Assemble the Tarts: Place 1 tablespoon of grape jam in the center of each piece of pastry, leaving a small border around the edges. Fold over the edges slightly to create a crust and prevent the jam from leaking.
4. Egg Wash and Sprinkle: Brush the edges of each tart with the beaten egg and sprinkle with granulated sugar.
5. Bake: Transfer the tarts to the prepared baking sheet and bake for 15–18 minutes, or until the pastry is golden and puffed.
6. Serve: Let cool slightly before serving. These are best enjoyed warm or at room temperature.

Tip: Add a dollop of whipped cream or a sprinkle of powdered sugar for extra flair.

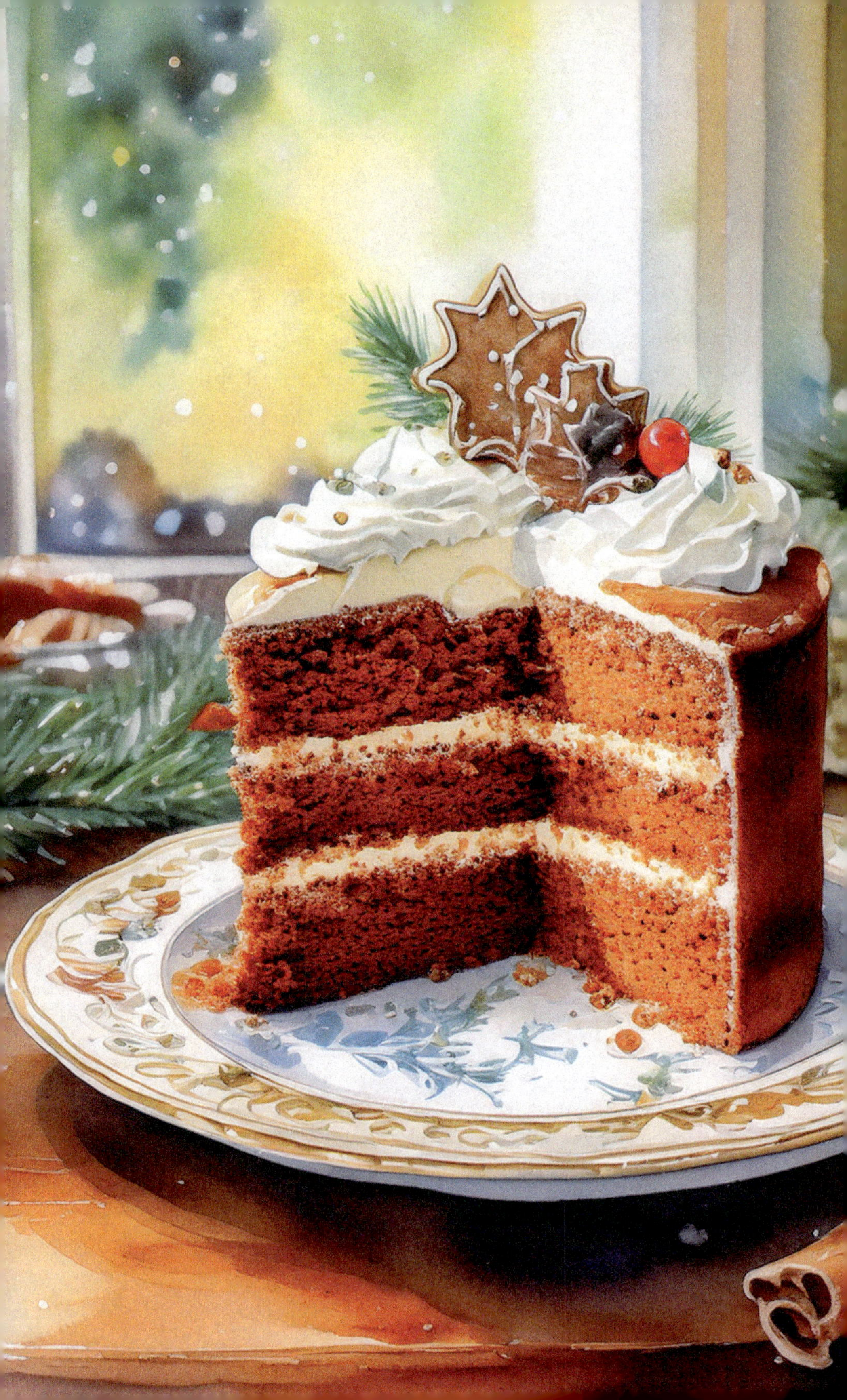

# Gingerbread Cake with Whipped Cream

This warmly spiced cake is a quintessential Victorian dessert, perfect for cozy winter evenings at the March home.

Ingredients:
- 1/2 cup unsalted butter, melted
- 1/2 cup molasses
- 1/2 cup brown sugar
- 1 large egg
- 1 teaspoon vanilla extract
- 1 1/2 cups all-purpose flour
- 1 teaspoon ground ginger
- 1 teaspoon cinnamon
- 1/2 teaspoon baking soda
- 1/2 cup boiling water

Instructions:
1. Prepare the Batter: Mix melted butter, molasses, sugar, egg, and vanilla. Stir in dry ingredients alternately with boiling water.
2. Bake: Pour into a greased 9-inch pan and bake at 350°F (175°C) for 30–35 minutes.
3. Serve: Cool slightly and serve with freshly whipped cream.

# Chapter 5: Festive Feasts and Celebrations

The holidays are a time to gather, reflect, and celebrate the simple joys of life—just as the March family did in Little Women. I've always imagined their festive meals filled with warmth, laughter, and the kind of dishes that bring everyone together. From the comforting flavors of Thanksgiving to the cheerful indulgence of Fourth of July desserts, this chapter captures the spirit of celebration with recipes that feel both timeless and special. These are the dishes I'd love to serve my own family during holidays, inspired by the traditions that shaped the March family's memorable moments.

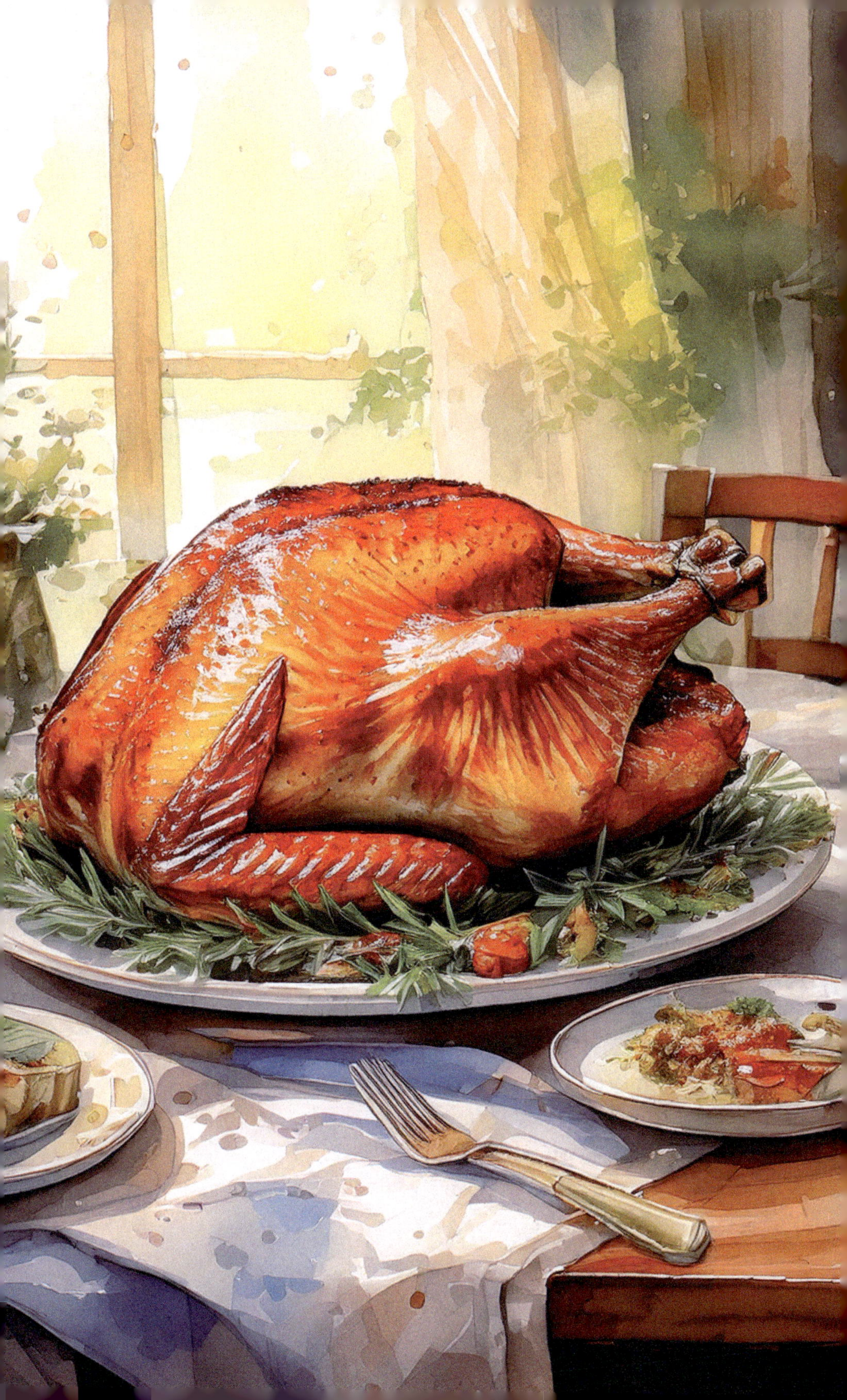

# Thanksgiving Turkey with Sage Stuffing

Thanksgiving was a time of reflection and gratitude in the March household. This roasted turkey with sage stuffing embodies the simplicity and heartiness of a traditional holiday meal.

Serves: 8–10

Ingredients for the Turkey:
- 12–14 lb whole turkey, thawed if frozen
- 1/2 cup unsalted butter, softened
- 2 teaspoons kosher salt
- 1 teaspoon ground black pepper
- 1 tablespoon fresh sage, chopped
- 1 teaspoon dried thyme
- 1 lemon, halved
- 1 onion, quartered
- 4 cups chicken or turkey broth (for basting)

Ingredients for the Stuffing:
- 10 cups cubed day-old bread (white or whole wheat)
- 1/2 cup unsalted butter
- 1 large onion, diced
- 2 celery stalks, diced
- 1 tablespoon fresh sage, chopped (or 1 teaspoon dried)
- 1 teaspoon dried thyme
- 1/2 teaspoon salt
- 1/2 teaspoon black pepper
- 1 1/2 cups chicken or turkey broth

Instructions:
1. Prepare the Turkey: Preheat the oven to 325°F (165°C). Pat the turkey dry with paper towels. Rub softened butter all over the turkey and under the skin. Season with salt, pepper, sage, and thyme. Stuff the cavity with lemon halves and onion quarters.
2. Make the Stuffing: Melt butter in a large skillet. Add onion and celery, cooking until softened. Toss with bread cubes, sage, thyme, salt, and pepper. Moisten with broth until just damp. Spoon loosely into the turkey cavity or bake separately in a greased dish for 30 minutes.
3. Roast the Turkey: Place the turkey in a roasting pan, breast side up. Add broth to the bottom of the pan. Cover loosely with foil and roast for 3–4 hours, basting every 30 minutes. Remove foil in the last hour to brown the skin. The turkey is done when a thermometer inserted into the thickest part of the thigh reads 165°F (74°C).
4. Rest and Serve: Let the turkey rest for 20 minutes before carving. Serve with stuffing and gravy.

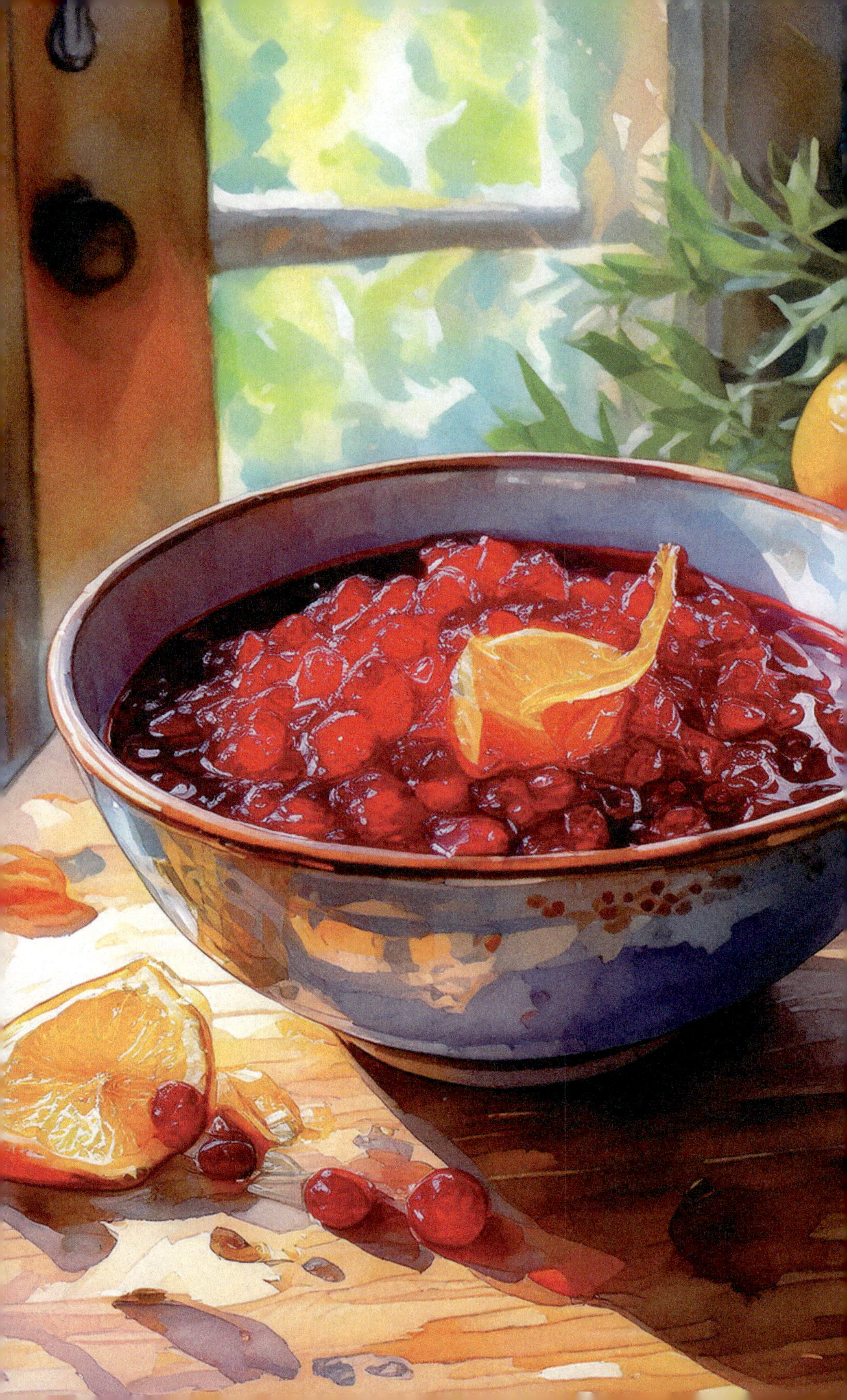

# Cranberry Sauce with Orange Zest

This bright and tangy cranberry sauce adds a festive touch to any Thanksgiving or Christmas table. The orange zest elevates its flavor, reflecting the resourcefulness of the March family.

Serves: 6

Ingredients:
- 12 oz fresh or frozen cranberries
- 3/4 cup granulated sugar
- 1/2 cup orange juice (freshly squeezed preferred)
- Zest of 1 orange

Instructions:
1. Cook the Cranberries: In a medium saucepan, combine cranberries, sugar, orange juice, and zest. Cook over medium heat, stirring occasionally, until the cranberries burst and the mixture thickens, about 10 minutes.
2. Cool and Serve: Remove from heat and let cool to room temperature. Refrigerate for at least 2 hours before serving.

Tip: Make ahead for better flavor; it keeps for up to 5 days in the refrigerator.

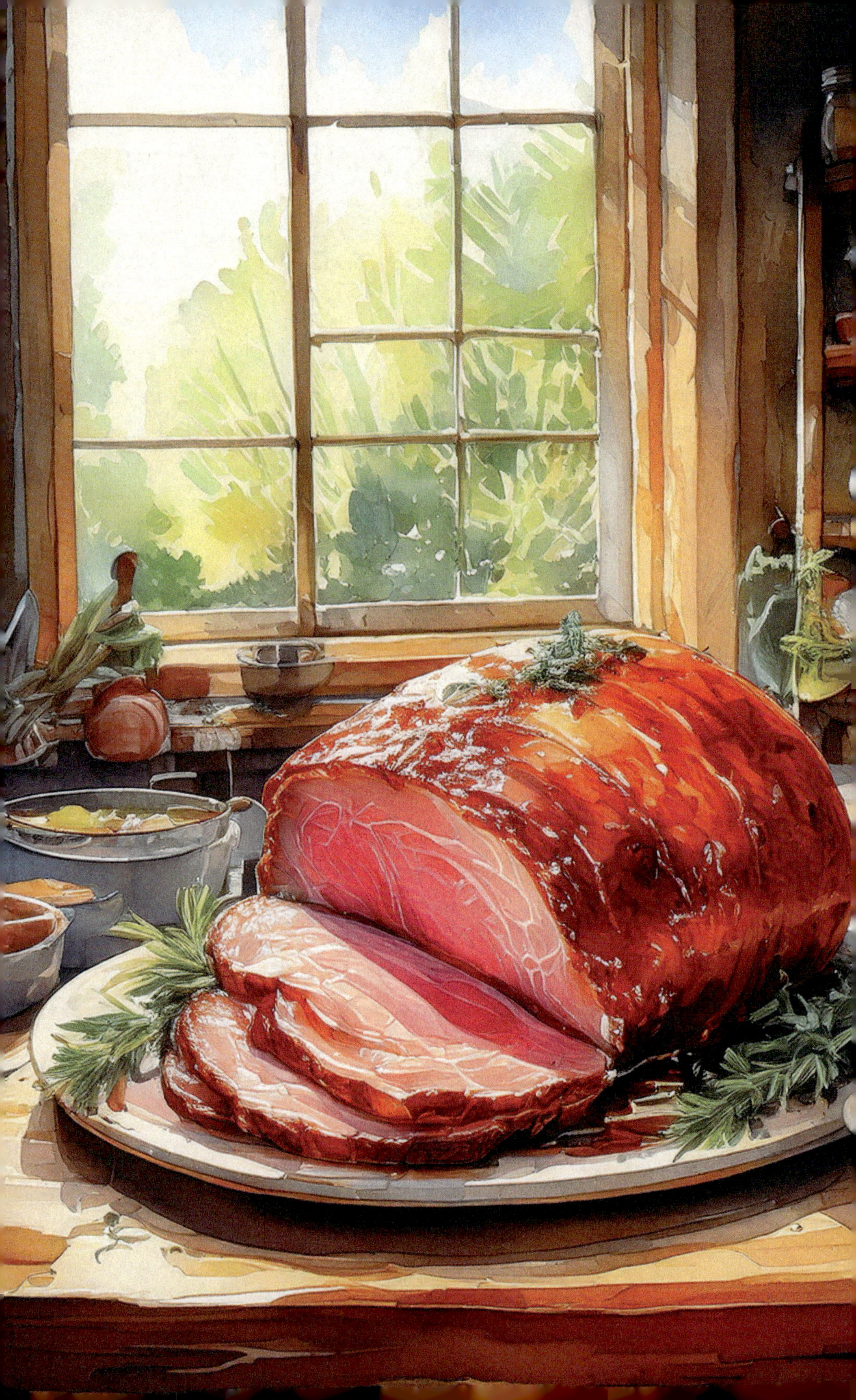

# Christmas Honey-Glazed Ham

Connection to Little Women: A honey-glazed ham reflects the warmth and abundance of a Victorian holiday feast. It's a perfect substitute for roast beef and brings a touch of sweetness to the Christmas table.

Serves: 8–10

Ingredients:
- 1 fully cooked, bone-in ham (8–10 pounds)
- 1 cup honey
- 1/2 cup brown sugar, packed
- 2 tablespoons Dijon mustard
- 1 teaspoon ground cinnamon
- 1/2 teaspoon ground cloves
- 1/4 teaspoon ground nutmeg
- 1/4 cup apple cider (or orange juice)

Instructions:
1. Preheat the Oven: Preheat your oven to 325°F (165°C). Place the ham on a rack in a large roasting pan, cut side down. Score the surface of the ham in a diamond pattern.
2. Make the Glaze: In a small saucepan, combine the honey, brown sugar, Dijon mustard, cinnamon, cloves, nutmeg, and apple cider. Cook over medium heat, stirring, until the sugar dissolves and the mixture is smooth.
3. Bake the Ham: Brush a generous amount of the glaze over the ham. Cover loosely with foil and bake for 1 1/2 to 2 hours, basting with glaze every 30 minutes.
4. Finish the Glaze: During the last 15–20 minutes of baking, remove the foil and brush on the remaining glaze. Continue baking until the glaze is caramelized and the ham is heated through.
5. Serve: Let the ham rest for 10–15 minutes before slicing. Serve warm, garnished with fresh herbs or citrus slices if desired.

Tip: Pair with Cranberry Sauce with Orange Zest

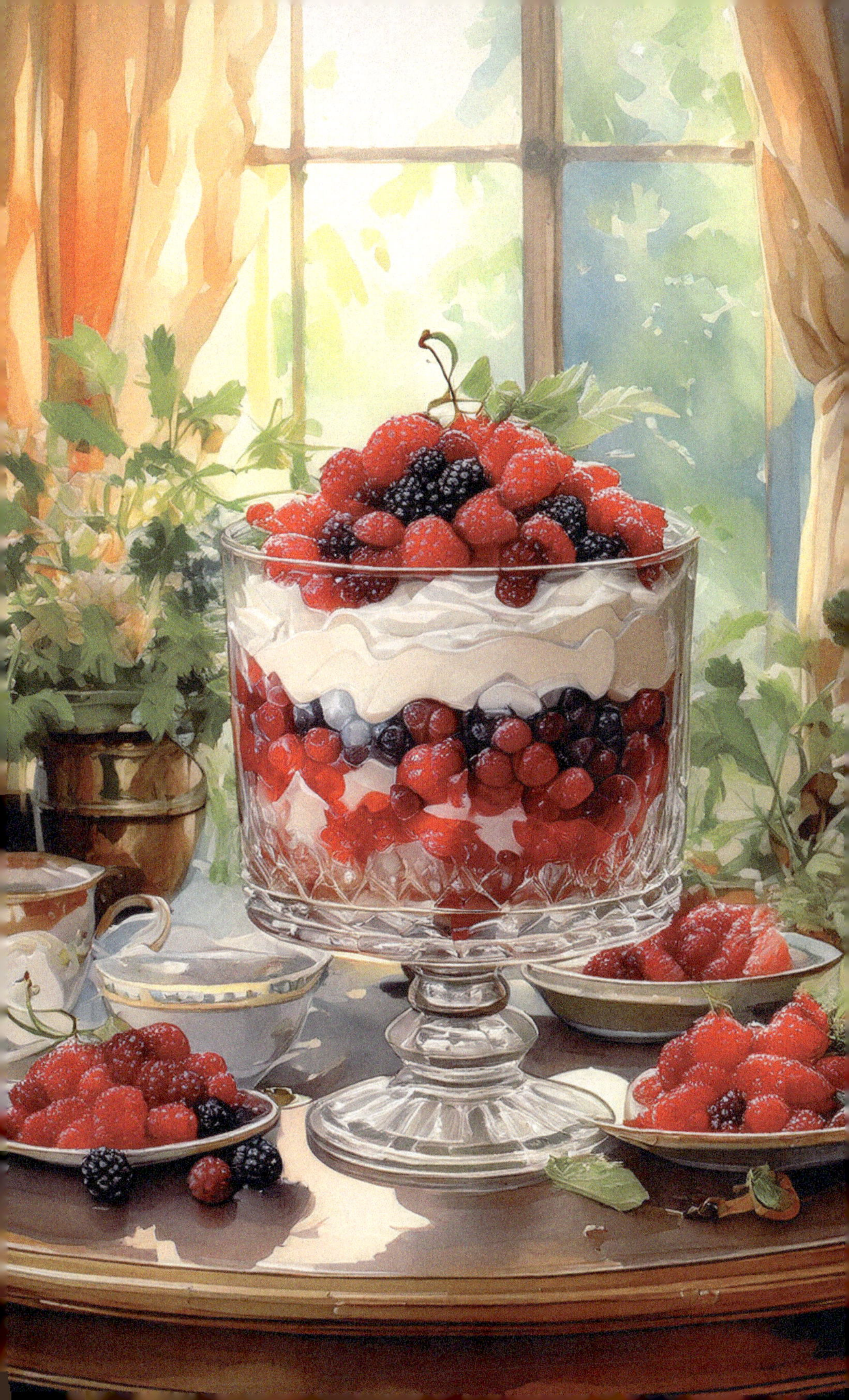

# Fourth of July Berry Trifle

This light and colorful dessert, layered with fresh berries and cream, reflects the festive spirit of Independence Day celebrations at Plumfield.

Ingredients for the Trifle:
- 1 angel food cake, cut into cubes
- 2 cups fresh strawberries, sliced
- 1 cup fresh blueberries
- 1 cup fresh raspberries

Ingredients for the Whipped Cream:
- 2 cups heavy cream, chilled
- 1/3 cup powdered sugar
- 1 teaspoon vanilla extract

Instructions:
1. Make the Whipped Cream:
   - In a large chilled mixing bowl, combine the heavy cream, powdered sugar, and vanilla extract.
   - Using a hand or stand mixer, whip on medium speed until soft peaks form. Be careful not to overwhip, as the cream can become grainy.
2. Assemble the Trifle:
   - In a large trifle dish or glass bowl, layer a third of the angel food cake cubes, followed by a third of the whipped cream, and a layer of mixed berries. Repeat the layers twice more, ending with a generous topping of whipped cream and a decorative arrangement of berries.
3. Chill and Serve:
   - Cover the trifle with plastic wrap and refrigerate for at least 1 hour before serving. This allows the flavors to meld beautifully.

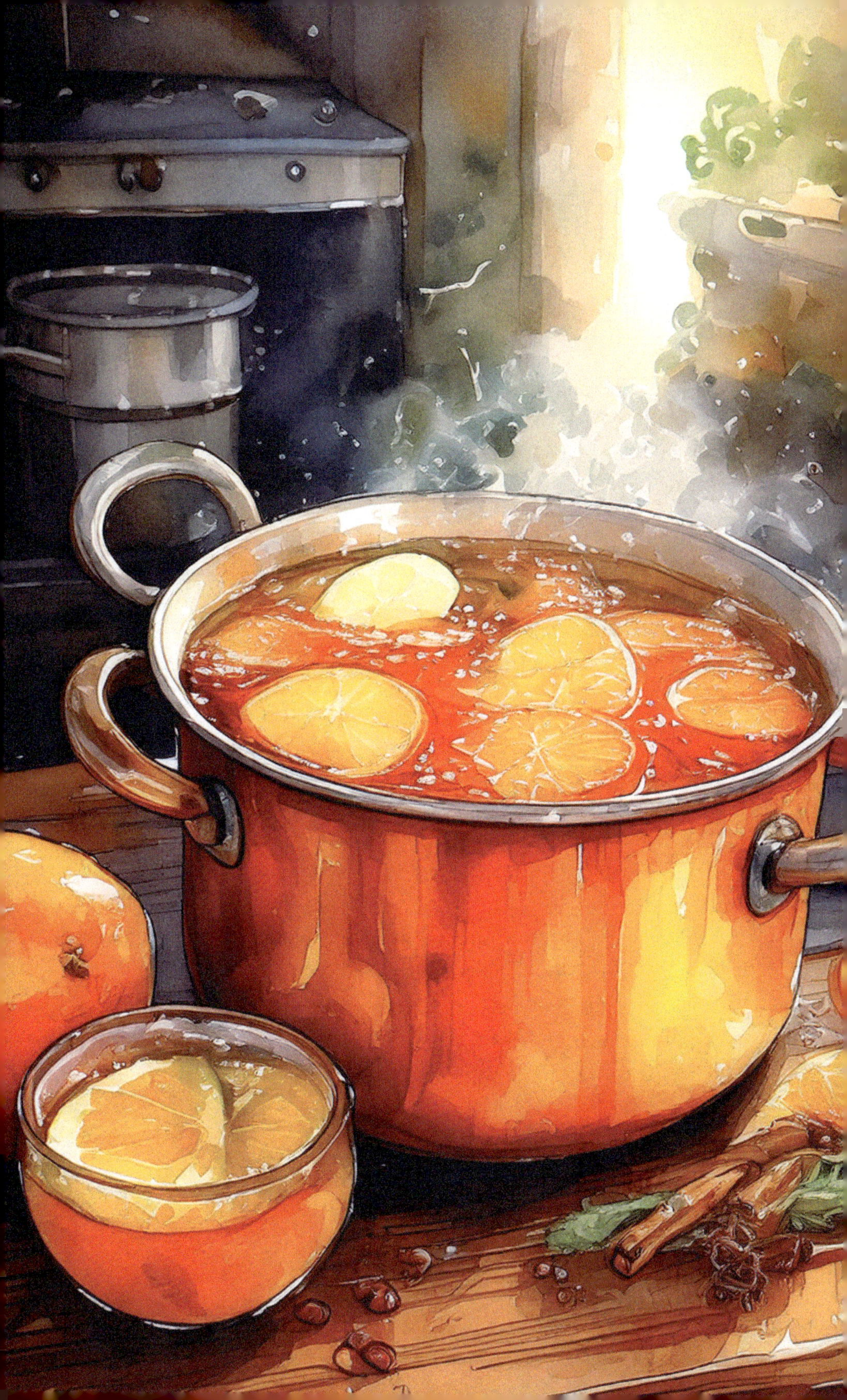

# New Year's Eve Wassail Punch

Wassail, a traditional spiced punch, would have been a warm and inviting drink for the March family's New Year's celebrations.

Serves: 8

Ingredients:
- 4 cups apple cider
- 2 cups orange juice
- 1/2 cup cranberry juice
- 1/4 cup brown sugar
- 1 cinnamon stick
- 4 whole cloves
- 1 orange, sliced
- Optional: 1/2 cup brandy or rum

Instructions:
1. Simmer the Punch: Combine all ingredients in a large pot. Simmer over low heat for 20–30 minutes, stirring occasionally.
2. Serve: Ladle into mugs and serve warm. Garnish with an orange slice or cinnamon stick.

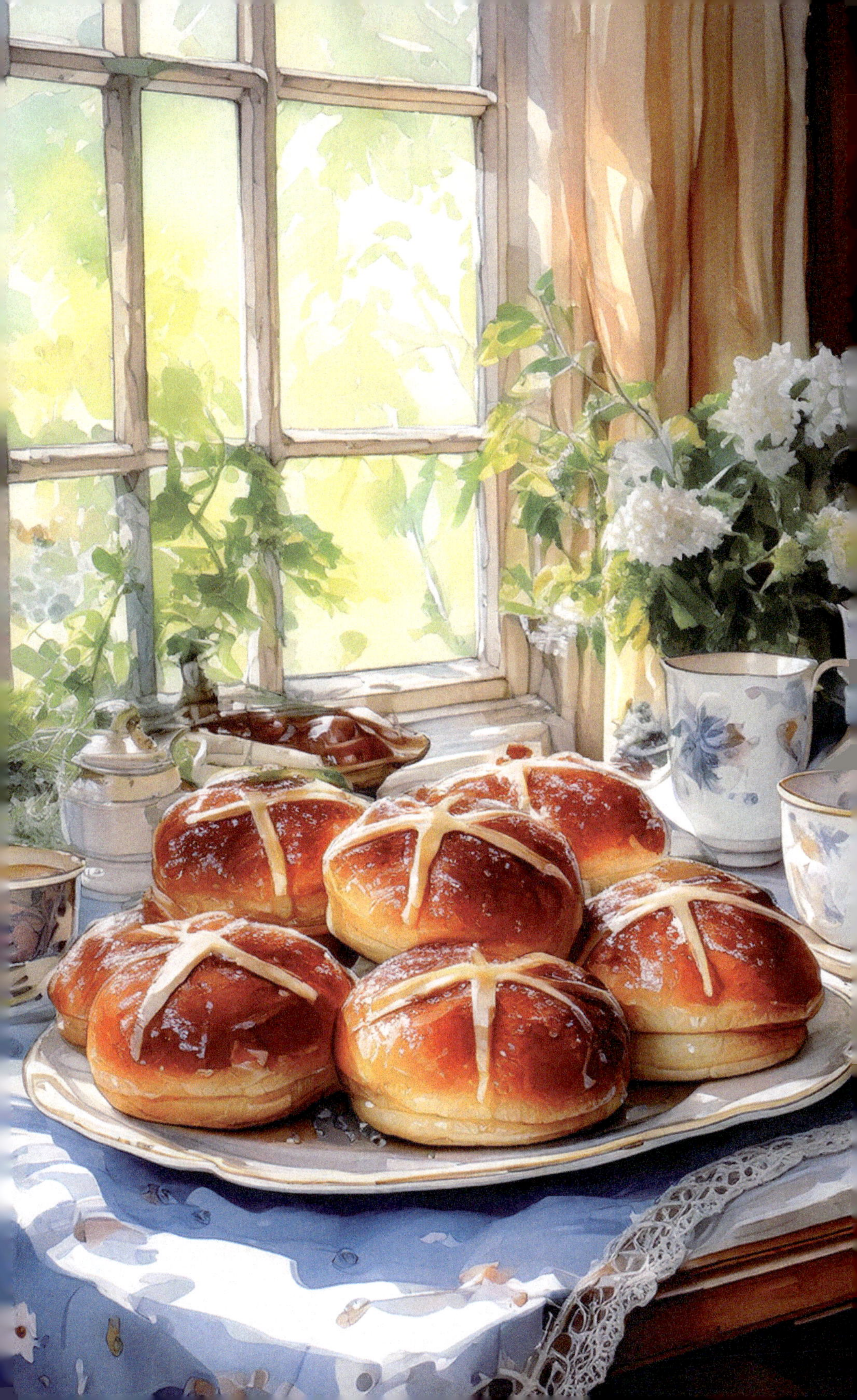

# Easter Hot Cross Buns

These spiced, slightly sweet buns, marked with a cross, are a traditional Easter treat. The March sisters would have enjoyed baking these to share with family and friends.

Serves: 12 buns

Ingredients:
- 1 cup warm milk (110°F/45°C)
- 2 1/4 teaspoons active dry yeast
- 1/4 cup granulated sugar
- 3 1/2 cups all-purpose flour
- 1 teaspoon ground cinnamon
- 1/2 teaspoon ground nutmeg
- 1/2 teaspoon salt
- 1/4 cup unsalted butter, melted
- 1 large egg
- 1/2 cup raisins

For the Crosses:
- 1/2 cup all-purpose flour
- 1/4 cup water

For the Glaze:
- 1/4 cup apricot jam, warmed

Instructions:
1. Make the Dough: Dissolve yeast in warm milk with 1 tablespoon sugar. Let sit until foamy, about 5 minutes. Combine flour, cinnamon, nutmeg, salt, remaining sugar, butter, egg, and raisins. Knead until smooth. Cover and let rise until doubled, about 1 hour.
2. Shape the Buns: Divide dough into 12 equal pieces, shape into balls, and place on a greased baking sheet. Cover and let rise for 30 minutes.
3. Add the Crosses: Mix flour and water to form a paste. Pipe a cross onto each bun.
4. Bake: Preheat oven to 375°F (190°C) and bake for 20–25 minutes, until golden. Brush with warmed apricot jam while still hot.

# Chapter 6:
# Tea Time Delights

Tea time has always been more than just a meal—it's a ritual, a pause in the day to connect with loved ones or indulge in a moment of quiet reflection. In Little Women, the March sisters bring their unique personalities to the tea table: Amy would delight in delicate and artistic creations, Meg would lean toward classic comforts, Beth might favor simple yet heartfelt treats, and Jo, practical as ever, might prefer something savory to balance the sweetness. This chapter captures the essence of Victorian tea time, blending timeless recipes with the spirit of the March family.

From the elegance of a Victoria sponge cake to the charm of raspberry thumbprint cookies, these recipes invite you to savor the joy of teatime. With both sweet and savory options, you can imagine yourself sharing these delights with the sisters as they discuss their dreams, challenges, and triumphs over a pot of tea. Each recipe is designed to transport you to a simpler, more intentional time, where every bite feels like an act of care and creativity.

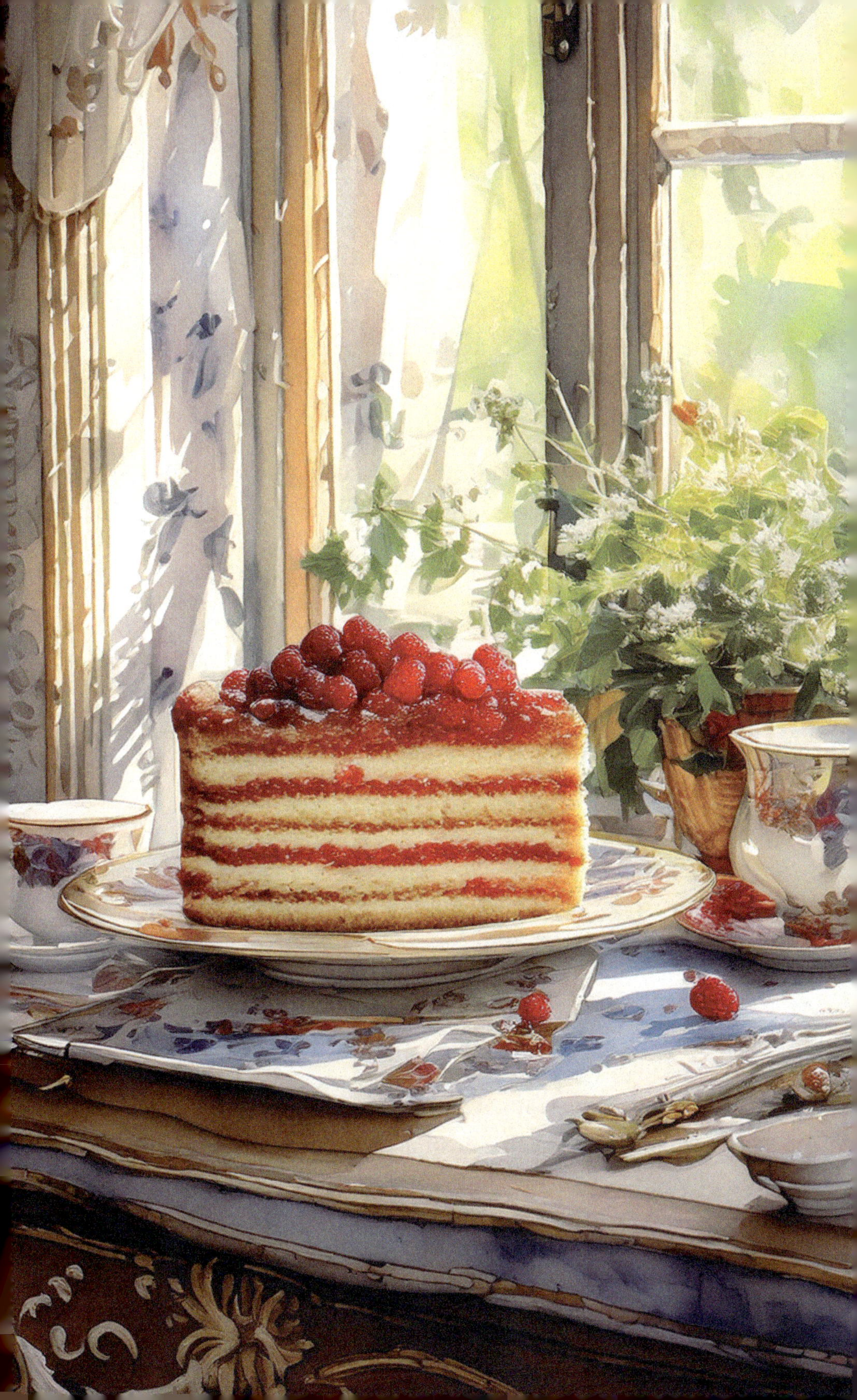

# Classic Victoria Sponge Cake

Named after Queen Victoria, this classic cake would have been a centerpiece for any elegant tea party. Its light sponge and sweet jam filling reflect the refinement Amy adored.

Serves: 8–10

Ingredients for the Cake:
- 1 cup unsalted butter, softened
- 1 cup granulated sugar
- 4 large eggs
- 2 cups self-rising flour
- 1 teaspoon vanilla extract
- 2 tablespoons milk

Ingredients for the Filling and Topping:
- 1/2 cup raspberry jam
- 1 cup heavy cream, whipped
- Powdered sugar, for dusting

Instructions:
1. Preheat the Oven: Preheat the oven to 350°F (175°C). Grease and line two 8-inch round cake pans.
2. Make the Batter: Cream the butter and sugar until light and fluffy. Beat in the eggs one at a time, followed by the vanilla. Gently fold in the flour, adding the milk to loosen the batter if needed.
3. Bake: Divide the batter evenly between the prepared pans and bake for 20–25 minutes, or until the cakes are golden and spring back when touched. Cool completely.
4. Assemble the Cake: Spread raspberry jam on one cake layer. Top with whipped cream, then place the second cake layer on top. Dust with powdered sugar before serving.

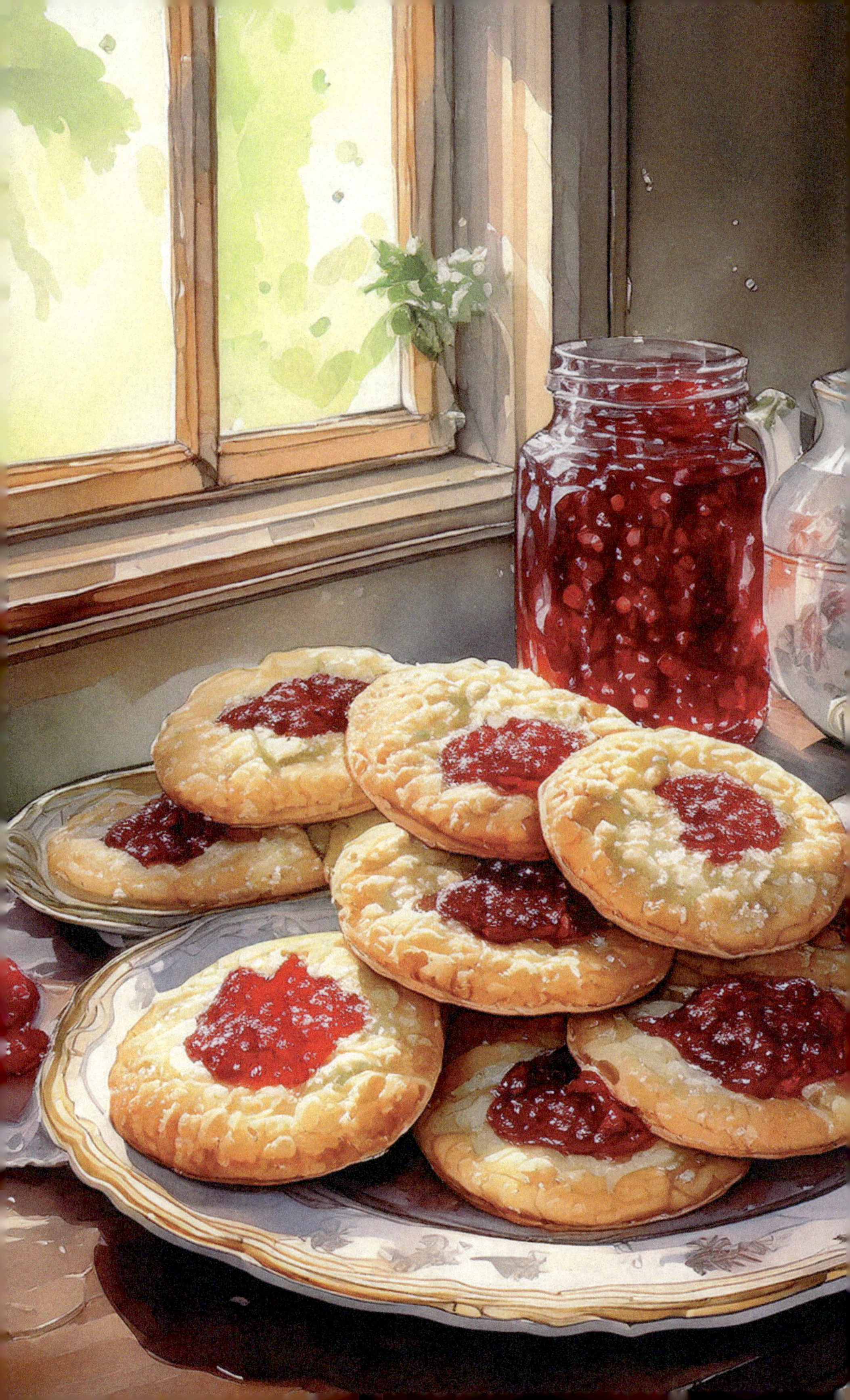

# Raspberry Thumbprint Cookies

These charming cookies are simple yet elegant, much like Meg's tea-time offerings for guests. The jewel-like raspberry centers add a touch of sophistication.

Makes: 24 cookies

Ingredients:
- 1 cup unsalted butter, softened
- 1/2 cup granulated sugar
- 2 cups all-purpose flour
- 1/2 teaspoon salt
- 1/3 cup raspberry jam

Instructions:
1. Preheat the Oven: Preheat your oven to 350°F (175°C). Line a baking sheet with parchment paper.
2. Make the Dough: Cream the butter and sugar until smooth. Gradually add the flour and salt, mixing until a soft dough forms.
3. Shape the Cookies: Roll the dough into 1-inch balls and place on the prepared baking sheet. Use your thumb or the back of a spoon to make an indentation in the center of each ball.
4. Add the Jam: Fill each indentation with a small amount of raspberry jam.
5. Bake: Bake for 12–15 minutes, or until the edges are lightly golden. Cool on a wire rack before serving.

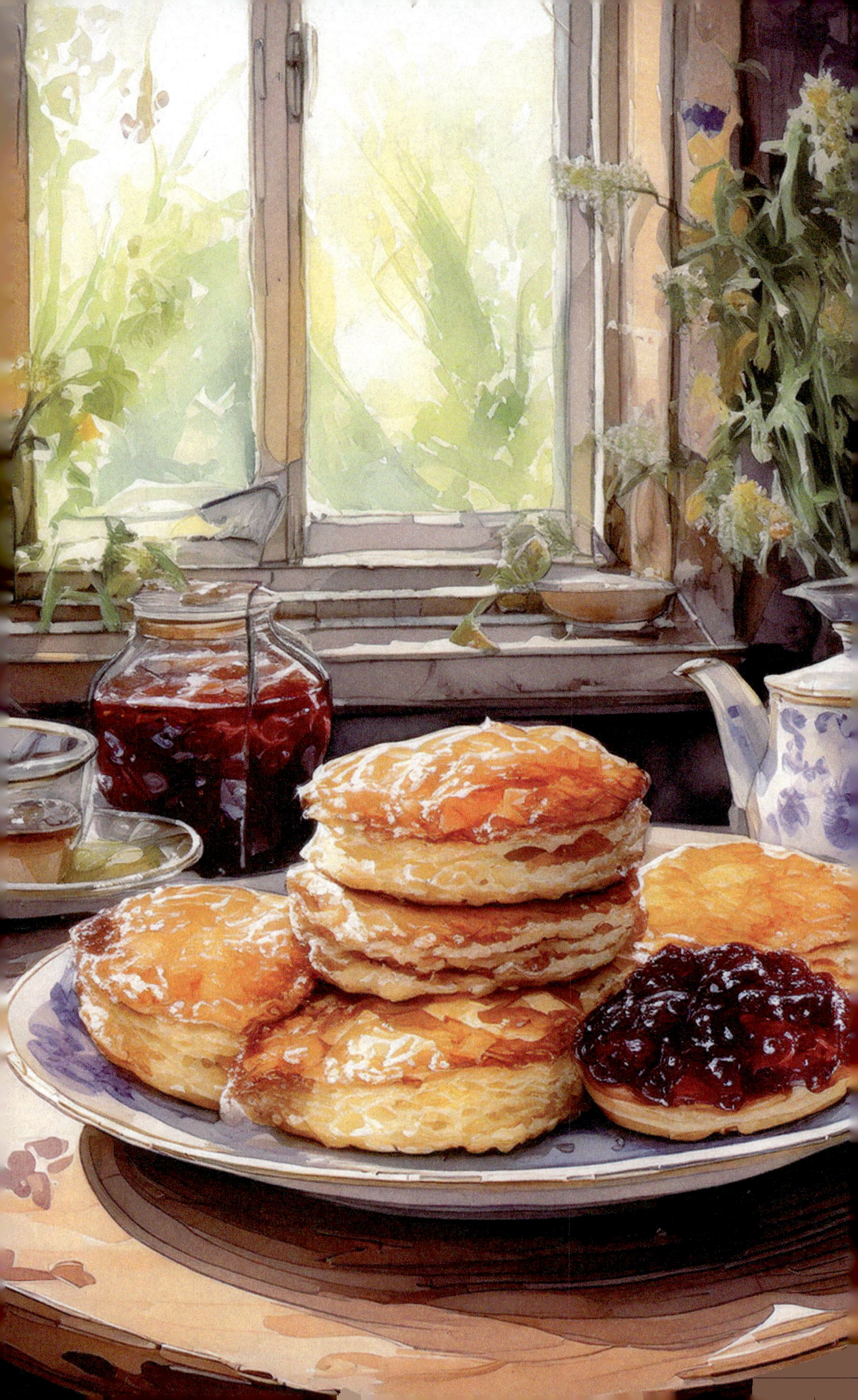

# Devonshire Cream Scones

These buttery scones pair perfectly with tea and jam, bringing a traditional English touch to the March family's tea table.

Makes: 8 scones

Ingredients:
- 2 cups all-purpose flour
- 2 teaspoons baking powder
- 1/4 teaspoon salt
- 1/4 cup granulated sugar
- 1/2 cup unsalted butter, chilled and cubed
- 1/2 cup whole milk
- 1 large egg, beaten (for brushing)

Instructions:
1. Preheat the Oven: Preheat your oven to 400°F (200°C). Line a baking sheet with parchment paper.
2. Make the Dough: In a large bowl, whisk together the flour, baking powder, salt, and sugar. Cut in the butter until the mixture resembles coarse crumbs. Gradually stir in the milk until the dough comes together.
3. Shape the Scones: Turn the dough onto a floured surface and gently knead. Pat into a 1-inch-thick round and cut into 8 wedges. Place on the prepared baking sheet.
4. Bake: Brush the tops with beaten egg and bake for 12–15 minutes, or until golden. Serve warm with clotted cream and jam.

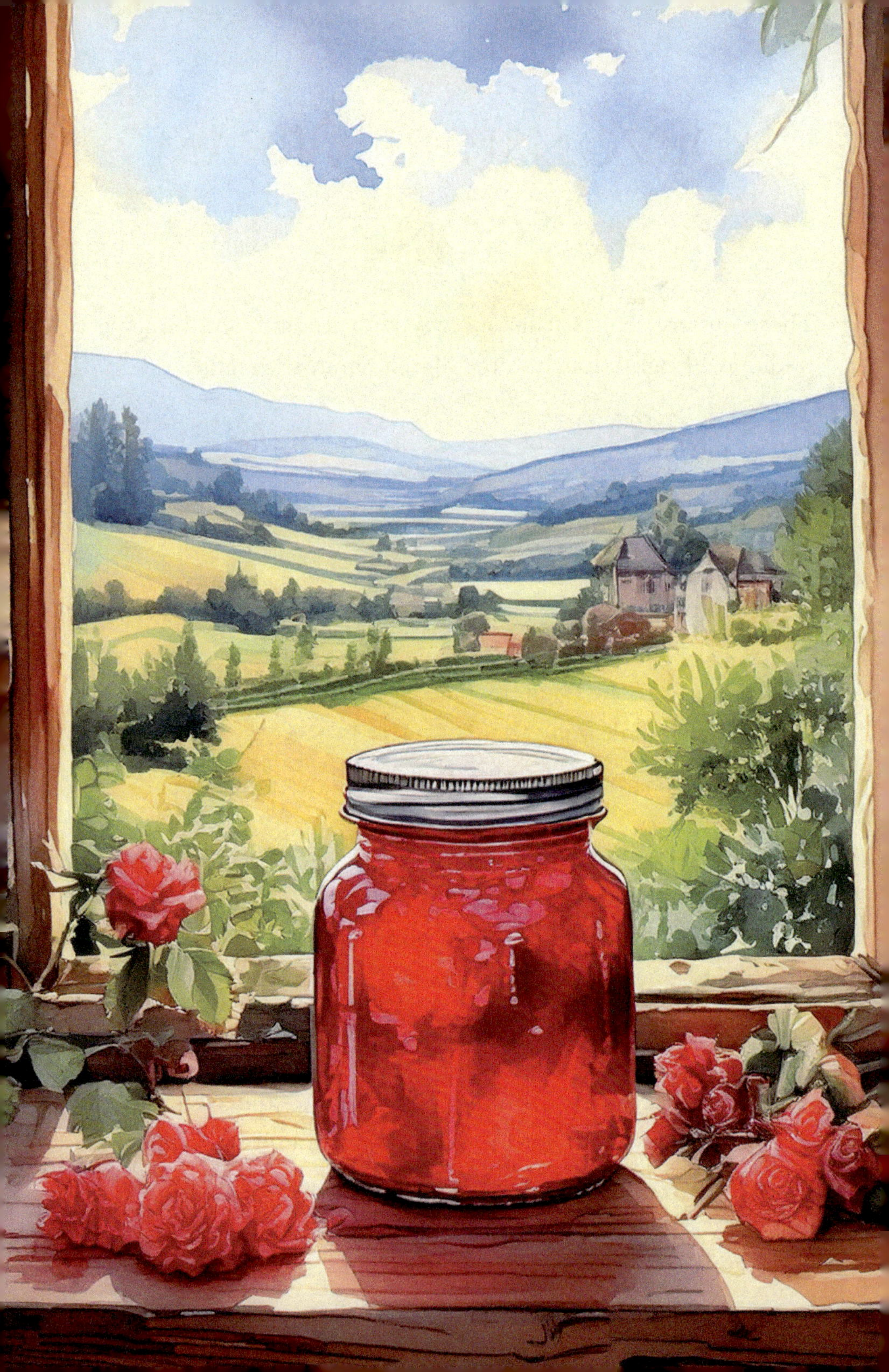

# Amy's Rose Petal Jam

Amy's love for beauty and refinement shines in this delicate jam, made with fragrant rose petals for a truly luxurious touch.

Ingredients:
- 1 cup fresh, unsprayed rose petals, washed and dried
- 2 cups granulated sugar
- 1/2 cup water
- 1 tablespoon lemon juice

Instructions:
1. Prepare the Syrup: In a medium saucepan, combine the sugar, water, and lemon juice. Bring to a boil, stirring until the sugar dissolves.
2. Add the Rose Petals: Reduce the heat and stir in the rose petals. Simmer for 15–20 minutes, or until the mixture thickens.
3. Jar the Jam: Pour into sterilized jars, seal, and let cool. Store in the refrigerator and use within a month.

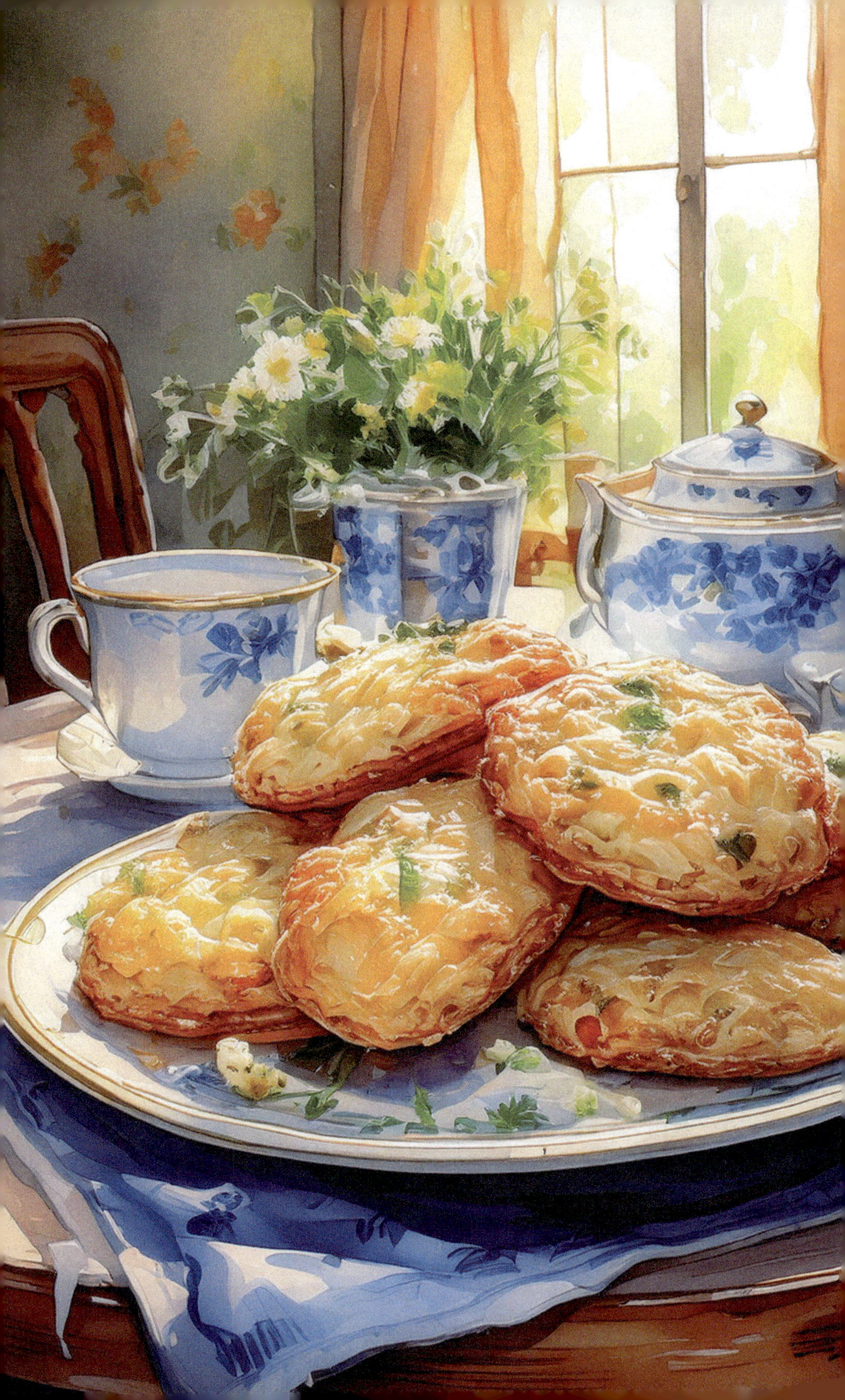

# Savory Cheese and Chive Biscuits

These savory biscuits bring balance to the sweetness of tea-time treats, much like Jo's no-nonsense attitude complements the gentler sides of her sisters.

Makes: 12 biscuits

Ingredients:
- 2 cups all-purpose flour
- 2 teaspoons baking powder
- 1/2 teaspoon salt
- 1/2 teaspoon garlic powder
- 1/2 cup unsalted butter, chilled and cubed
- 1 cup shredded cheddar cheese
- 2 tablespoons chopped fresh chives
- 3/4 cup buttermilk

Instructions:
1. Preheat the Oven: Preheat your oven to 400°F (200°C). Line a baking sheet with parchment paper.
2. Make the Dough: In a large bowl, whisk together the flour, baking powder, salt, and garlic powder. Cut in the butter until the mixture resembles coarse crumbs. Stir in the cheese and chives. Add the buttermilk and mix until just combined.
3. Shape and Bake: Drop spoonfuls of dough onto the baking sheet and bake for 12–15 minutes, or until golden. Serve warm.

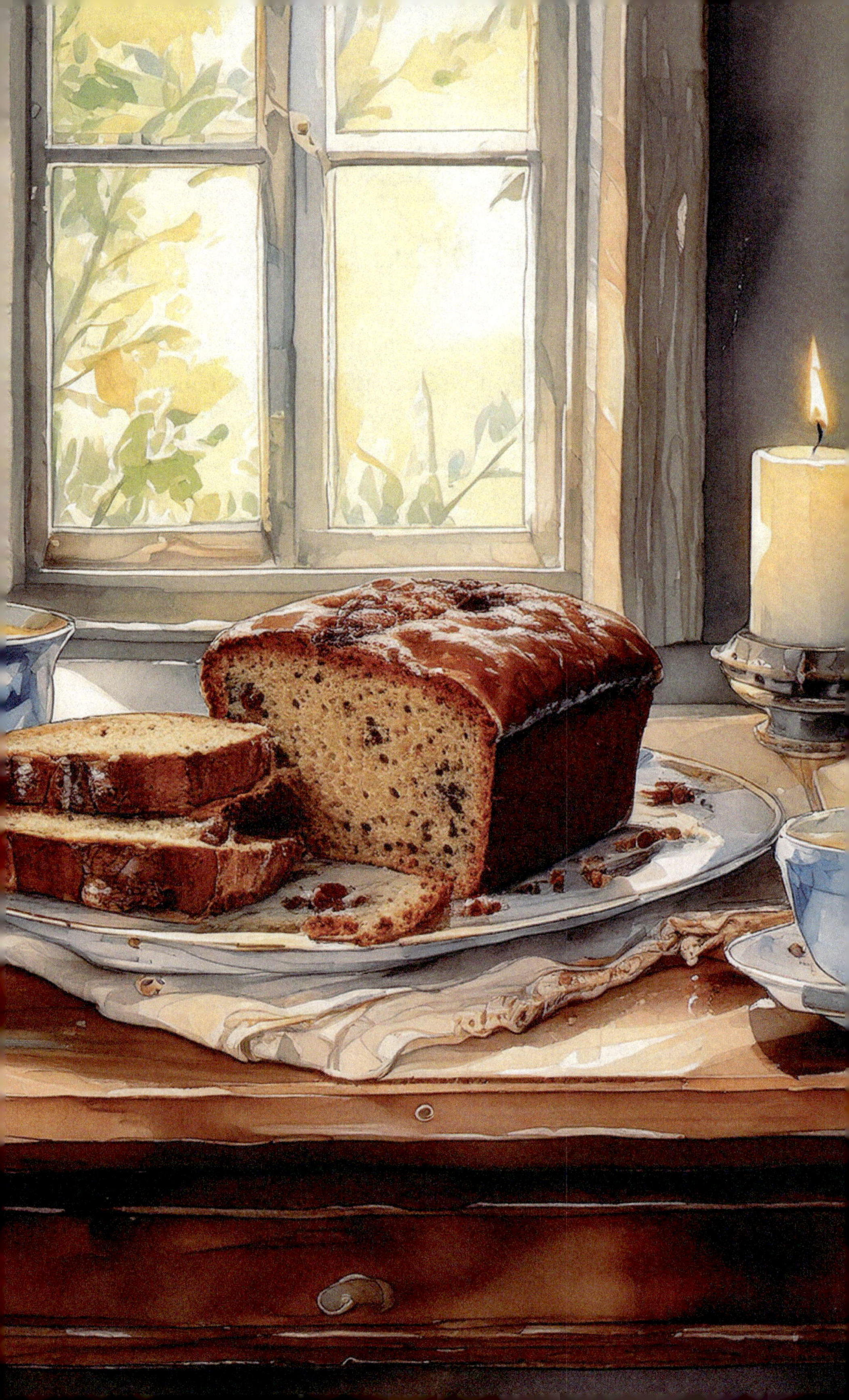

# Earl Grey Tea Loaf

This fragrant tea loaf, infused with Earl Grey, reflects the simple pleasures of tea time—a moment of calm in the March family's busy household.

Serves: 8

Ingredients:
- 2 Earl Grey tea bags
- 1 cup boiling water
- 1/2 cup unsalted butter, melted
- 1/2 cup brown sugar, packed
- 1 large egg
- 2 cups all-purpose flour
- 2 teaspoons baking powder
- 1/2 teaspoon ground cinnamon
- 1/4 teaspoon salt
- 1/2 cup golden raisins

Instructions:
1. Steep the Tea: Place the tea bags in a cup and pour over the boiling water. Let steep for 10 minutes. Remove the bags and let the tea cool.
2. Mix the Batter: In a large bowl, combine the butter, brown sugar, egg, and cooled tea. Stir in the flour, baking powder, cinnamon, and salt until just combined. Fold in the raisins.
3. Bake: Pour the batter into a greased loaf pan and bake at 350°F (175°C) for 40–45 minutes, or until a toothpick inserted into the center comes out clean.
4. Serve: Let cool before slicing. Enjoy plain or with butter.

# Chapter 7: Preserves and Pantry Staples

The art of preserving food was essential in the March family's time, not just for practicality but for adding a touch of flavor and luxury to their modest meals. Whether it's jars of jewel-toned jelly or tangy pickles, these pantry staples reflect the creativity and care that went into making the most of seasonal abundance.

This chapter celebrates the tradition of preserving, offering recipes that feel timeless yet approachable. From Amy's indulgent lemon curd to a classic spiced pear butter, these recipes will fill your pantry with flavors that elevate even the simplest meals.

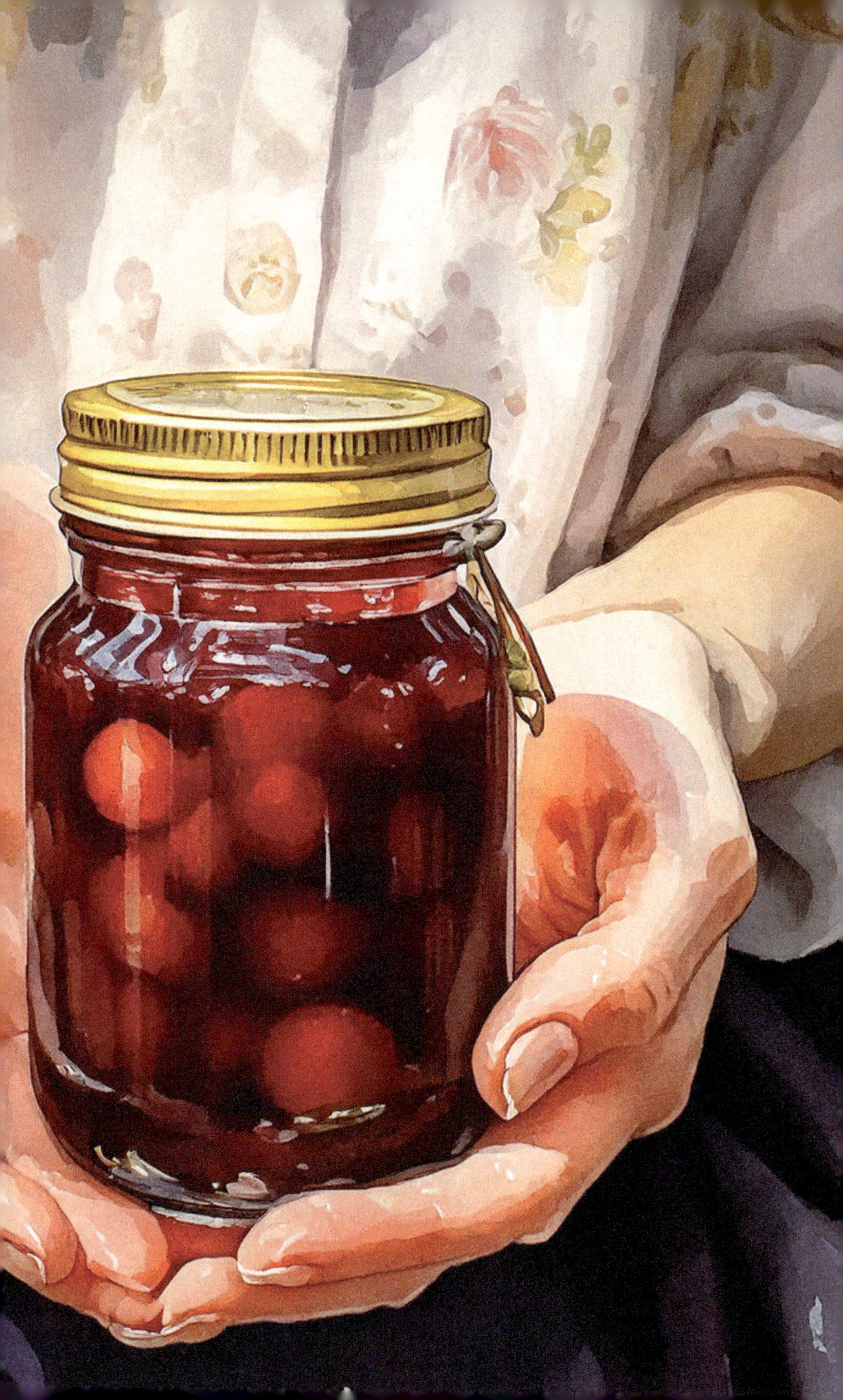

# Concord Grape Jelly

Concord grapes, native to Louisa May Alcott's hometown, make this jelly a fitting homage to her roots. This sweet, versatile preserve would have been a cherished addition to the March family's pantry.

Makes: About 4 cups

Ingredients:
- 4 pounds Concord grapes, washed and stems removed
- 1 cup water
- 4 cups granulated sugar
- 1 packet (1.75 oz) powdered fruit pectin

Instructions:
1. Cook the Grapes: In a large pot, combine the grapes and water. Bring to a boil, then reduce the heat and simmer for 10 minutes, mashing the grapes with a spoon.
2. Strain the Juice: Pour the mixture through a fine-mesh sieve or jelly bag into a bowl, pressing to extract as much juice as possible. You should have about 4 cups of juice.
3. Make the Jelly: Return the juice to the pot. Stir in the pectin and bring to a boil. Add the sugar and boil for 1–2 minutes, stirring constantly. Skim off any foam.
4. Jar the Jelly: Pour the hot jelly into sterilized jars, leaving 1/4-inch headspace. Seal and process in a boiling water bath for 10 minutes.

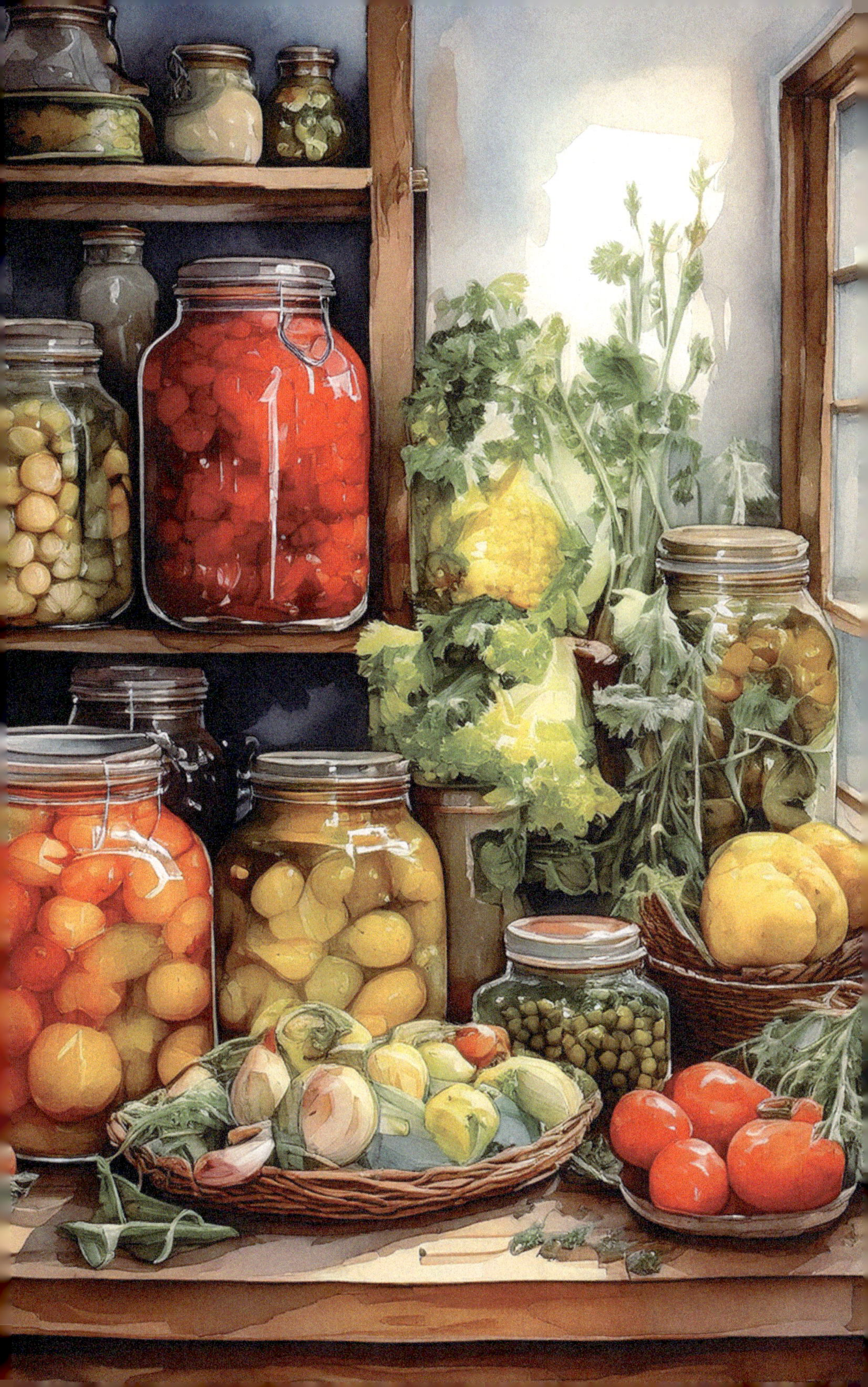

# Pickled Vegetables: A Taste of Preservation

Pickling was a practical way for families like the Marches to preserve fresh vegetables for winter. These crunchy, tangy pickles add zest to any meal.

Makes: 4 pints

Ingredients:
- 1 pound carrots, peeled and cut into sticks
- 1 pound green beans, trimmed
- 1 small head of cauliflower, cut into florets
- 4 cups white vinegar
- 4 cups water
- 1/4 cup kosher salt
- 2 tablespoons sugar
- 4 cloves garlic, peeled
- 2 teaspoons mustard seeds
- 2 teaspoons black peppercorns
- 1 teaspoon red pepper flakes (optional)

Instructions:
1. Prepare the Vegetables: Blanch the carrots, beans, and cauliflower in boiling water for 2 minutes. Drain and cool.
2. Make the Brine: In a large pot, combine the vinegar, water, salt, and sugar. Bring to a boil, stirring until dissolved.
3. Pack the Jars: Divide the garlic, mustard seeds, peppercorns, and red pepper flakes among 4 sterilized jars. Pack the vegetables tightly into the jars. Pour the hot brine over the vegetables, leaving 1/4-inch headspace.
4. Seal and Process: Seal the jars and process in a boiling water bath for 10 minutes. Let cool and store in a cool, dark place for at least 1 week before opening.

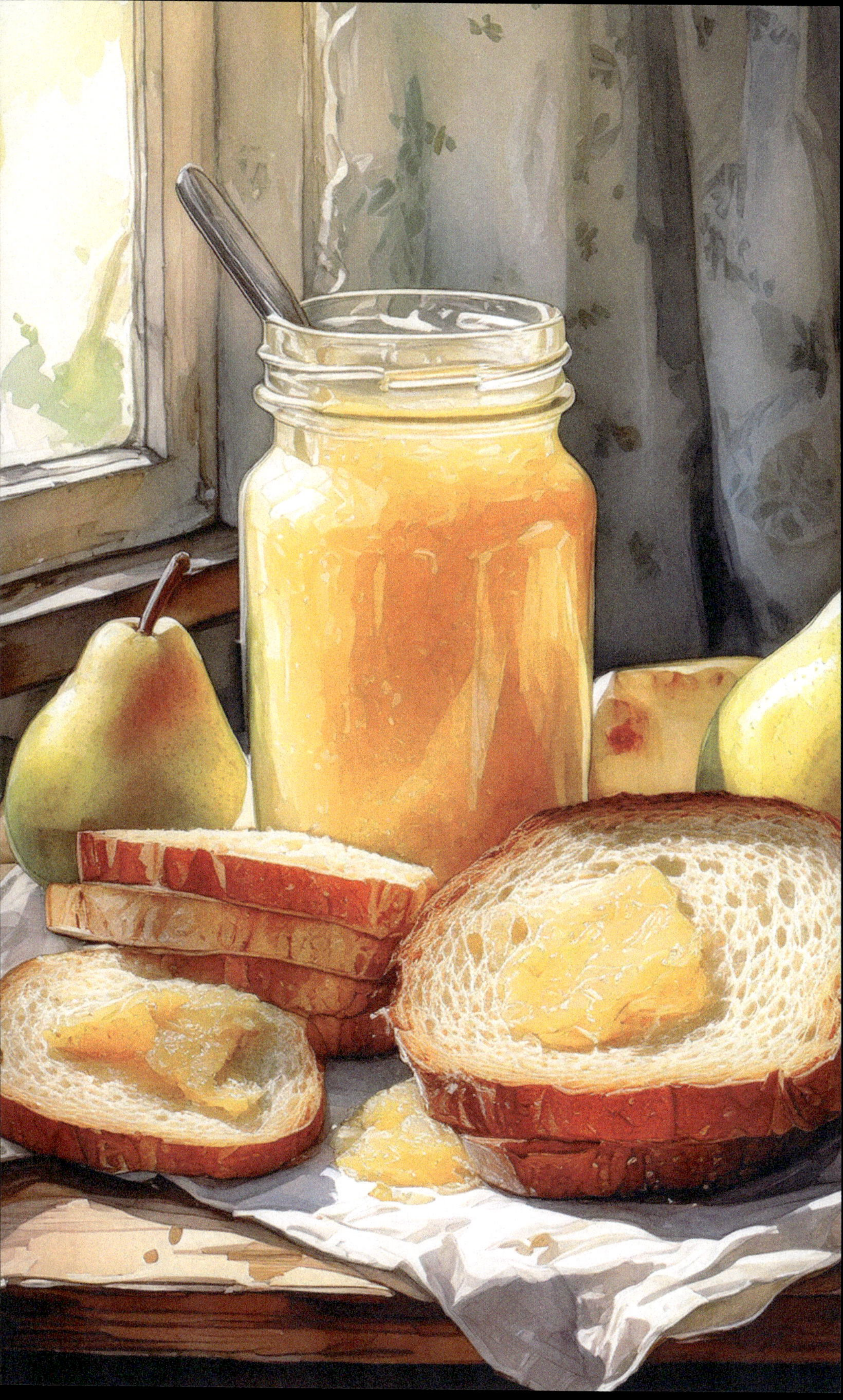

# Spiced Pear Butter

Pear butter captures the essence of fall, much like the quiet coziness of the March household during the cooler months.

Makes: About 4 cups

Ingredients:
- 4 pounds ripe pears, peeled, cored, and diced
- 1 cup granulated sugar
- 1/2 cup brown sugar
- 1 teaspoon ground cinnamon
- 1/2 teaspoon ground nutmeg
- 1/4 teaspoon ground cloves
- 1 tablespoon lemon juice

Instructions:
1. Cook the Pears: In a large pot, combine the pears, sugars, spices, and lemon juice. Cook over medium heat, stirring occasionally, until the pears are soft, about 30 minutes.
2. Blend and Thicken: Puree the mixture using an immersion blender or regular blender until smooth. Return to the pot and simmer on low, stirring frequently, until thickened, about 1 hour.
3. Jar the Pear Butter: Spoon into sterilized jars, leaving 1/4-inch headspace. Seal and process in a boiling water bath for 10 minutes.

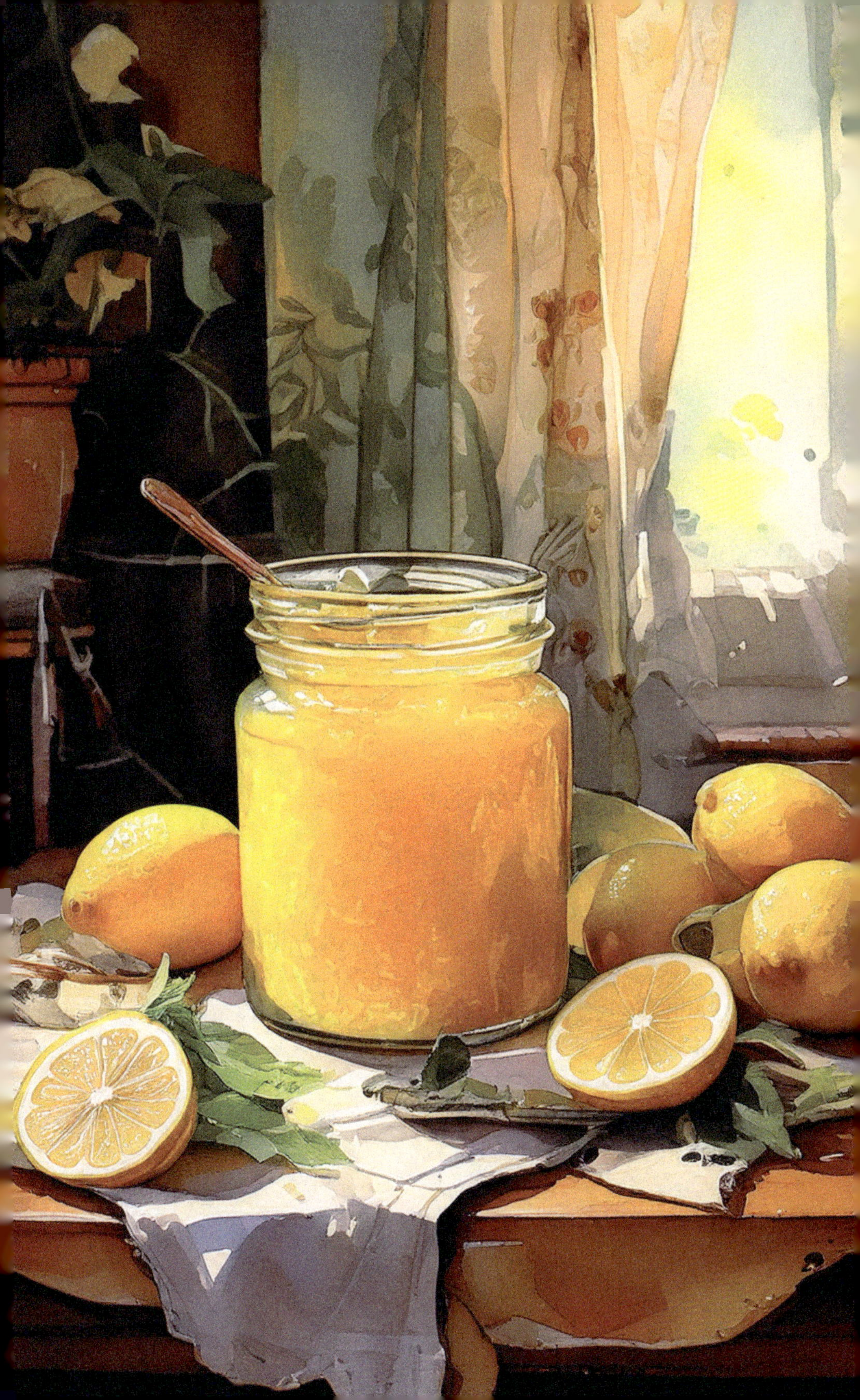

# Amy's Fancy Lemon Curd

This velvety lemon curd is as indulgent and elegant as Amy herself. Spread it on scones or use it as a filling for tarts to bring a touch of sophistication to any occasion.

Makes: About 2 cups

Ingredients:
- 3 large eggs
- 1 cup granulated sugar
- 1/2 cup fresh lemon juice (about 3 lemons)
- Zest of 2 lemons
- 6 tablespoons unsalted butter, cubed

Instructions:
1. Cook the Curd: In a heatproof bowl set over a pot of simmering water, whisk together the eggs, sugar, lemon juice, and zest. Cook, whisking constantly, until thickened, about 8–10 minutes.
2. Add the Butter: Remove from heat and whisk in the butter until smooth.
3. Store: Pour into sterilized jars and cool completely before refrigerating. Use within 2 weeks.

# Chapter 8: Everyday Comforts

In the world of Little Women, the simple joys of everyday life are often found around the dinner table. Whether it's a hearty stew on a chilly evening or a warm cider after a day of hard work, these recipes evoke the comfort and coziness of the March household. Each dish in this chapter is inspired by the resourcefulness and warmth of the family's meals, designed to bring a sense of home to your table.

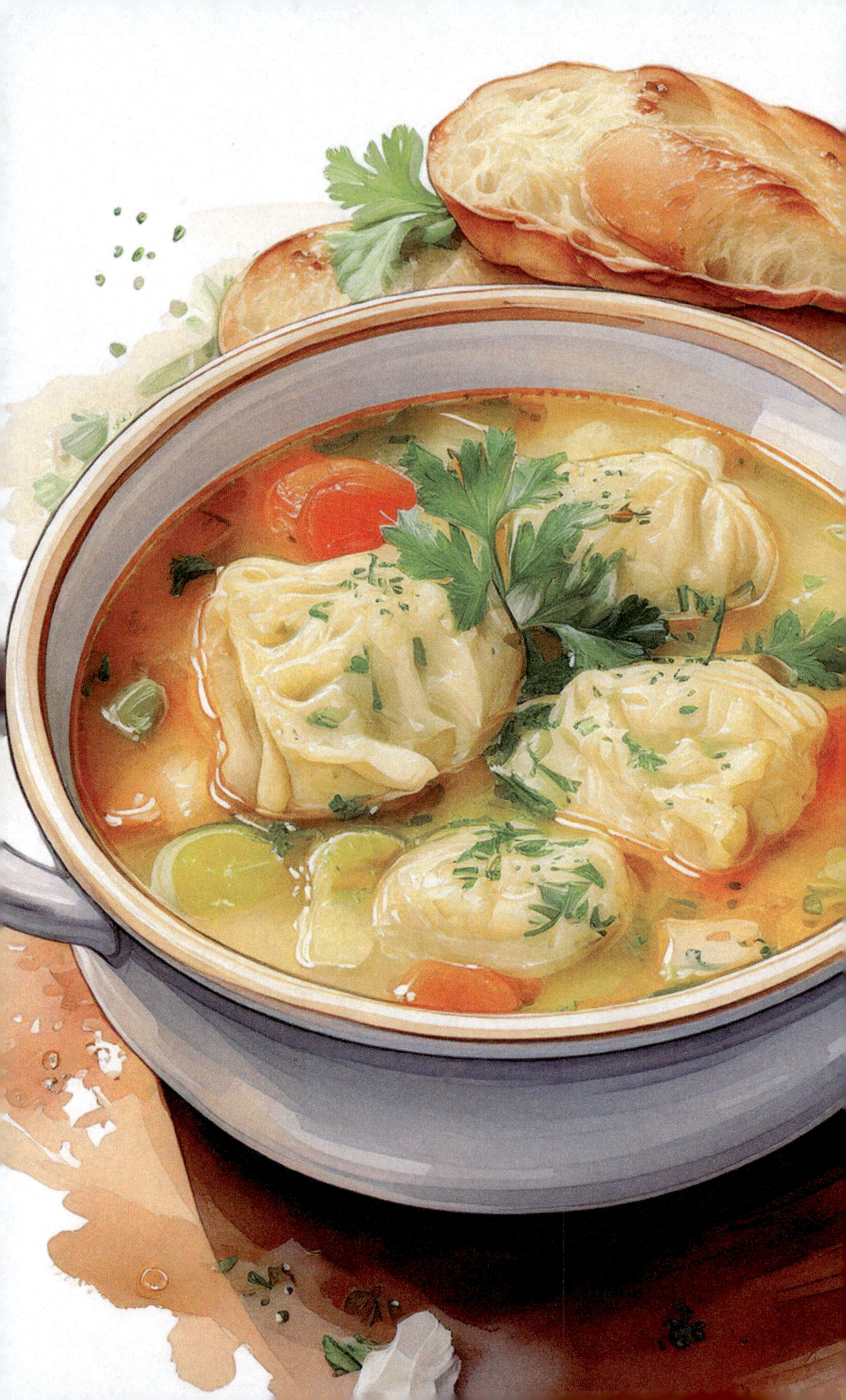

# Chicken and Dumplings

This comforting dish, with its tender chicken and fluffy dumplings, reflects the March family's ability to turn simple ingredients into a meal that nourishes both body and soul.

Serves: 6

Ingredients for the Chicken Stew:
- 2 tablespoons olive oil
- 1 medium onion, diced
- 2 celery stalks, diced
- 2 carrots, sliced
- 3 cloves garlic, minced
- 6 cups chicken broth
- 2 cups cooked chicken, shredded
- 1 teaspoon dried thyme
- 1 bay leaf
- Salt and pepper, to taste

Ingredients for the Dumplings:
- 1 1/2 cups all-purpose flour
- 1 tablespoon baking powder
- 1/2 teaspoon salt
- 1/2 cup whole milk
- 3 tablespoons unsalted butter, melted

Instructions:
1. Make the Stew: Heat olive oil in a large pot over medium heat. Add onion, celery, and carrots, and sauté until softened. Stir in garlic and cook for 1 minute. Add chicken broth, chicken, thyme, bay leaf, salt, and pepper. Bring to a simmer.
2. Prepare the Dumplings: In a bowl, whisk together flour, baking powder, and salt. Stir in milk and melted butter until just combined.
3. Cook the Dumplings: Drop spoonfuls of dough onto the simmering stew. Cover and cook for 15–20 minutes, or until the dumplings are fluffy and cooked through.
4. Serve: Ladle into bowls and serve warm.

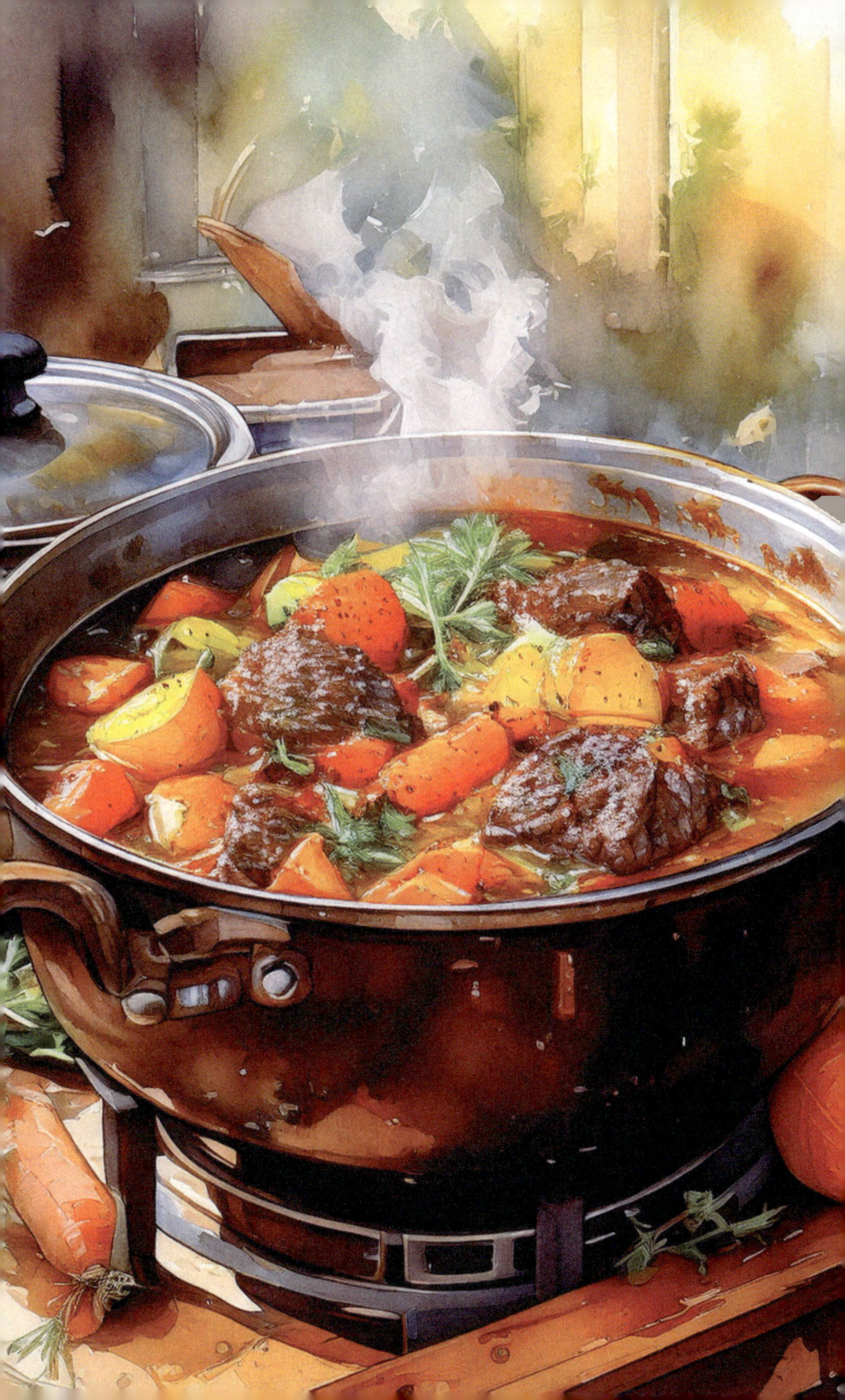

# Hearty Beef Stew with Root Vegetables

A slow-simmered stew like this would have been a staple in the March home during colder months, making the most of hearty vegetables and affordable cuts of meat.

Serves: 6

Ingredients:
- 2 tablespoons olive oil
- 2 pounds beef chuck, cut into 1-inch cubes
- 3 tablespoons all-purpose flour
- 1 teaspoon salt
- 1/2 teaspoon black pepper
- 1 medium onion, diced
- 3 garlic cloves, minced
- 4 cups beef broth
- 1 cup red wine (optional, or substitute with more broth)
- 2 carrots, peeled and sliced
- 2 parsnips, peeled and diced
- 1 large turnip, diced
- 1 teaspoon dried thyme
- 1 bay leaf

Instructions:
1. Brown the Beef: Toss the beef with flour, salt, and pepper. Heat olive oil in a large pot and brown the beef in batches. Remove and set aside.
2. Sauté the Aromatics: Add onion and garlic to the pot and cook until softened. Deglaze the pot with wine or a splash of broth, scraping up browned bits.
3. Simmer the Stew: Return the beef to the pot and add broth, carrots, parsnips, turnip, thyme, and bay leaf. Cover and simmer for 2 hours, or until the beef is tender.
4. Serve: Remove the bay leaf and serve with crusty bread.

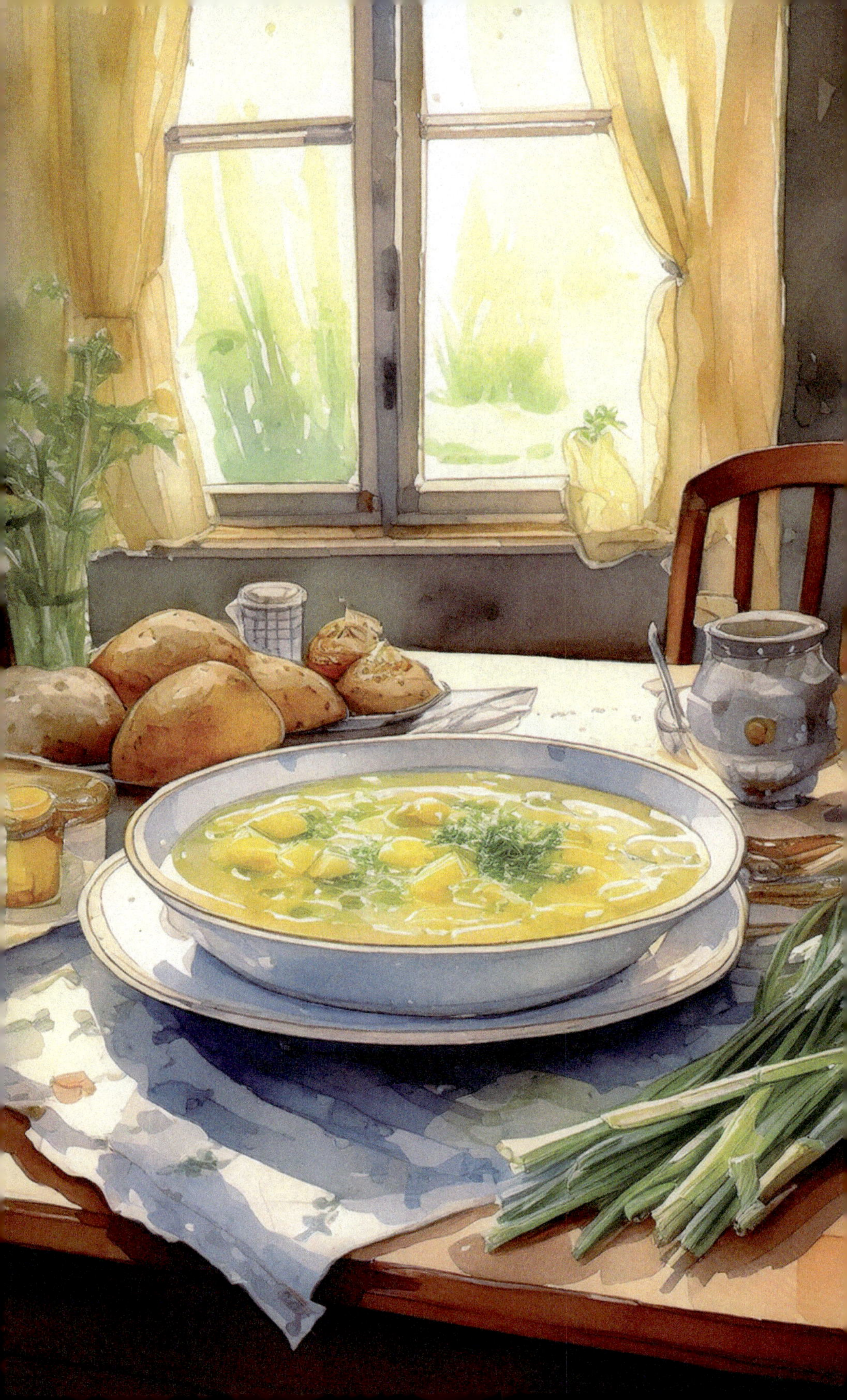

# Potato and Leek Soup

This simple and soothing soup is a nod to Beth's gentle, comforting nature—a dish perfect for quiet evenings by the fire.

Serves: 4–6

Ingredients:
- 2 tablespoons unsalted butter
- 2 leeks, white and light green parts only, sliced
- 4 cups peeled and diced potatoes
- 4 cups chicken or vegetable broth
- 1/2 cup heavy cream
- Salt and pepper, to taste

Instructions:
1. Sauté the Leeks: Melt butter in a large pot over medium heat. Add leeks and cook until softened, about 5 minutes.
2. Cook the Potatoes: Add potatoes and broth. Bring to a boil, then reduce heat and simmer until potatoes are tender, about 20 minutes.
3. Blend the Soup: Use an immersion blender or regular blender to puree the soup until smooth. Stir in heavy cream and season with salt and pepper.
4. Serve: Ladle into bowls and garnish with fresh herbs if desired.

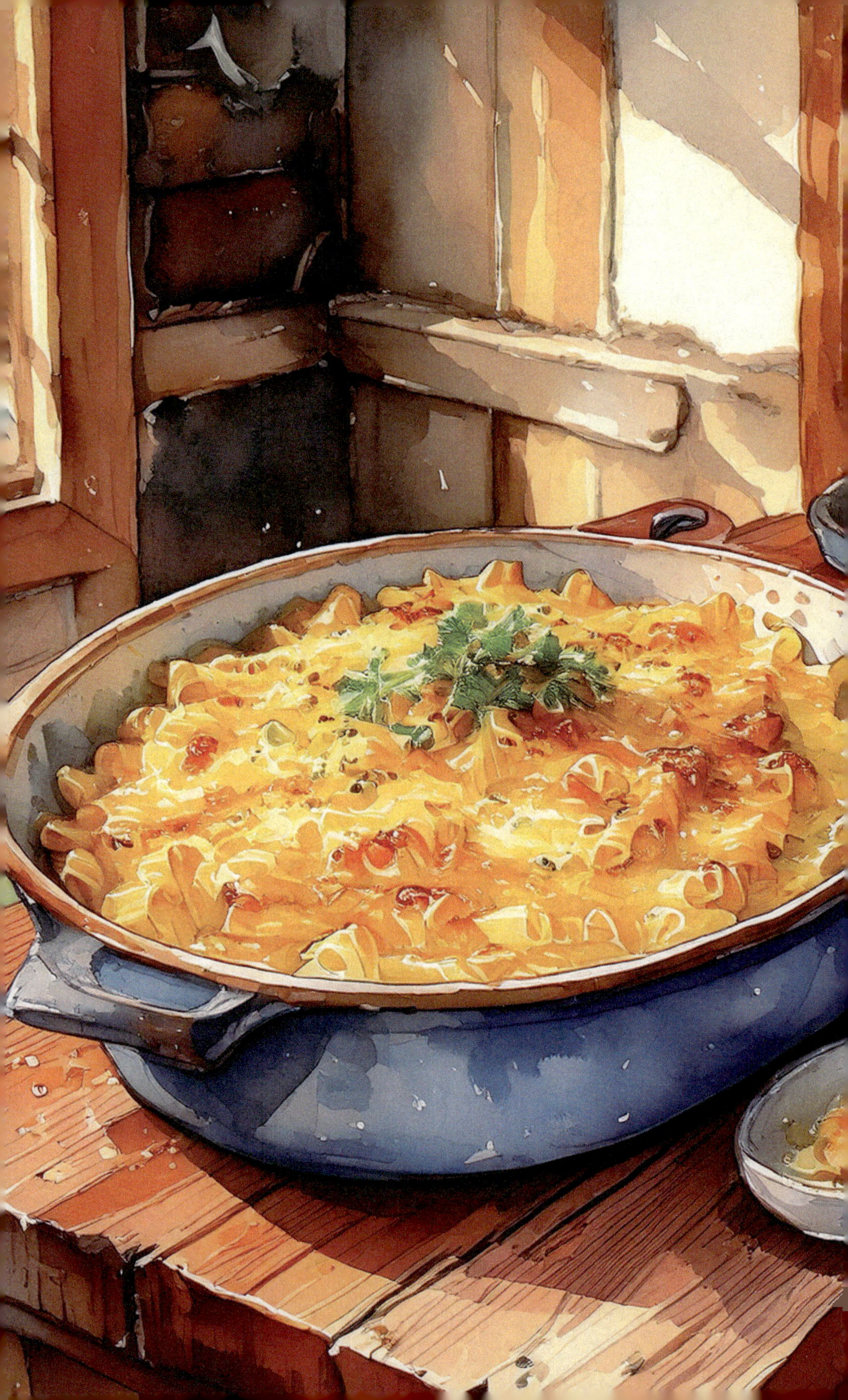

# Baked Macaroni with Cheese Crust

This indulgent dish, with its golden, cheesy crust, would have been a special treat for the March sisters, offering a rich and satisfying meal.

Serves: 6

Ingredients:
- 12 ounces elbow macaroni
- 4 tablespoons unsalted butter
- 1/4 cup all-purpose flour
- 3 cups whole milk
- 1/2 teaspoon salt
- 1/4 teaspoon black pepper
- 1/4 teaspoon ground mustard
- 2 cups shredded sharp cheddar cheese
- 1/2 cup breadcrumbs

Instructions:
1. Cook the Pasta: Preheat the oven to 375°F (190°C). Cook macaroni according to package instructions. Drain and set aside.
2. Make the Sauce: Melt butter in a saucepan. Whisk in flour and cook for 1–2 minutes. Gradually add milk, whisking constantly, until thickened. Stir in salt, pepper, mustard, and 1 1/2 cups cheese.
3. Assemble and Bake: Combine the sauce with the cooked macaroni and pour into a greased baking dish. Top with remaining cheese and breadcrumbs. Bake for 20–25 minutes, or until golden and bubbly.
4. Serve: Let cool slightly before serving.

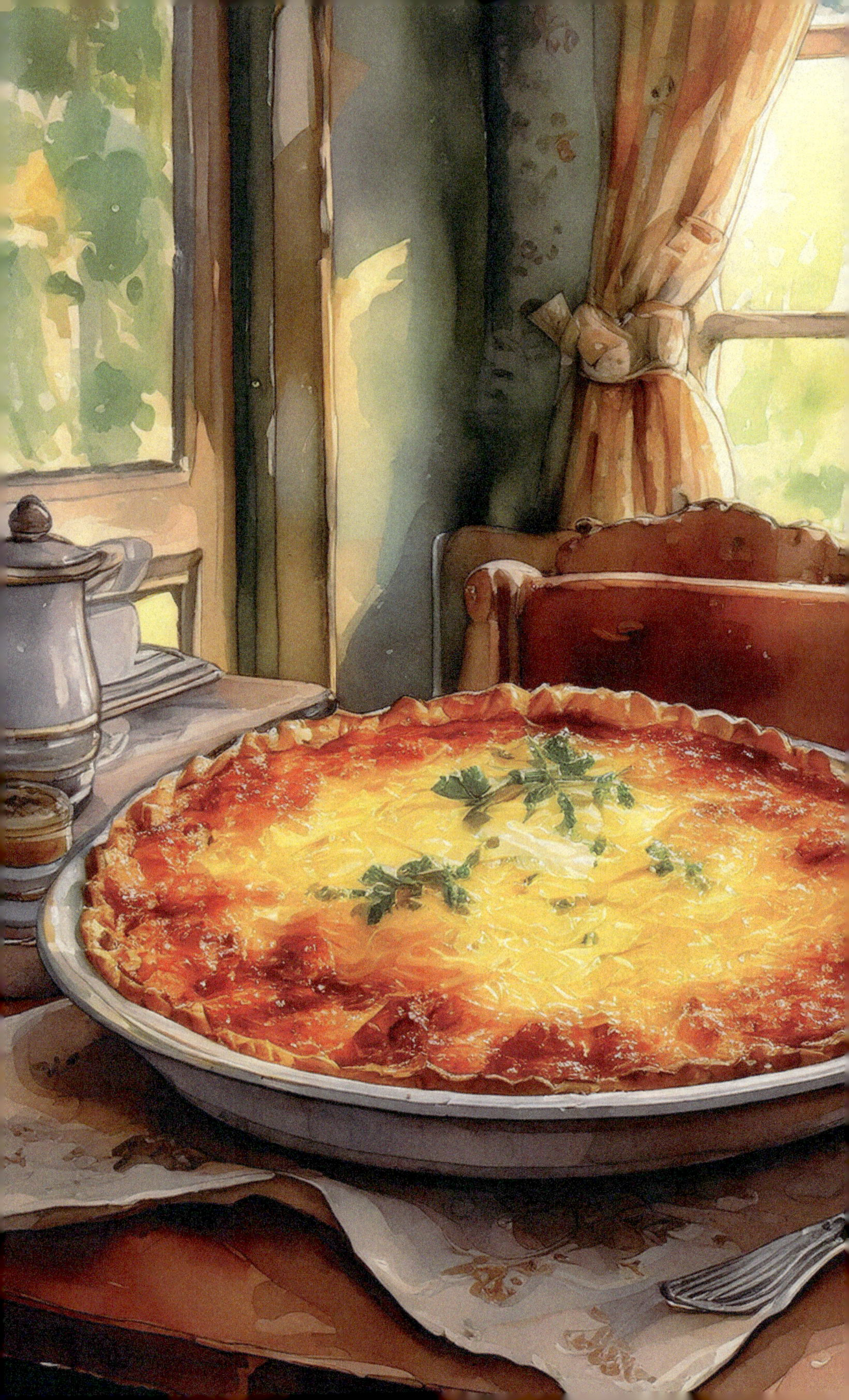

# Shepherd's Pie with Herbed Mash

This rustic dish is hearty and practical, much like Jo's approach to life. It combines simple ingredients into a meal that satisfies and comforts. Serves: 6

Ingredients for the Filling:
- 2 tablespoons olive oil
- 1 pound ground lamb or beef
- 1 onion, diced
- 2 carrots, diced
- 2 tablespoons tomato paste
- 1 cup beef or vegetable broth
- 1 teaspoon Worcestershire sauce
- 1 teaspoon dried thyme
- Salt and pepper, to taste

Ingredients for the Mash:
- 2 pounds potatoes, peeled and cubed
- 1/4 cup unsalted butter
- 1/2 cup whole milk
- 1 teaspoon chopped parsley
- Salt and pepper, to taste

Instructions:
1. Make the Filling: Heat olive oil in a skillet. Add ground meat, onion, and carrots, cooking until browned. Stir in tomato paste, broth, Worcestershire sauce, thyme, salt, and pepper. Simmer until thickened.
2. Prepare the Mash: Boil potatoes until tender. Drain and mash with butter, milk, parsley, salt, and pepper.
3. Assemble and Bake: Spread the filling in a baking dish. Top with mashed potatoes, spreading evenly. Bake at 375°F (190°C) for 25 minutes, or until golden.

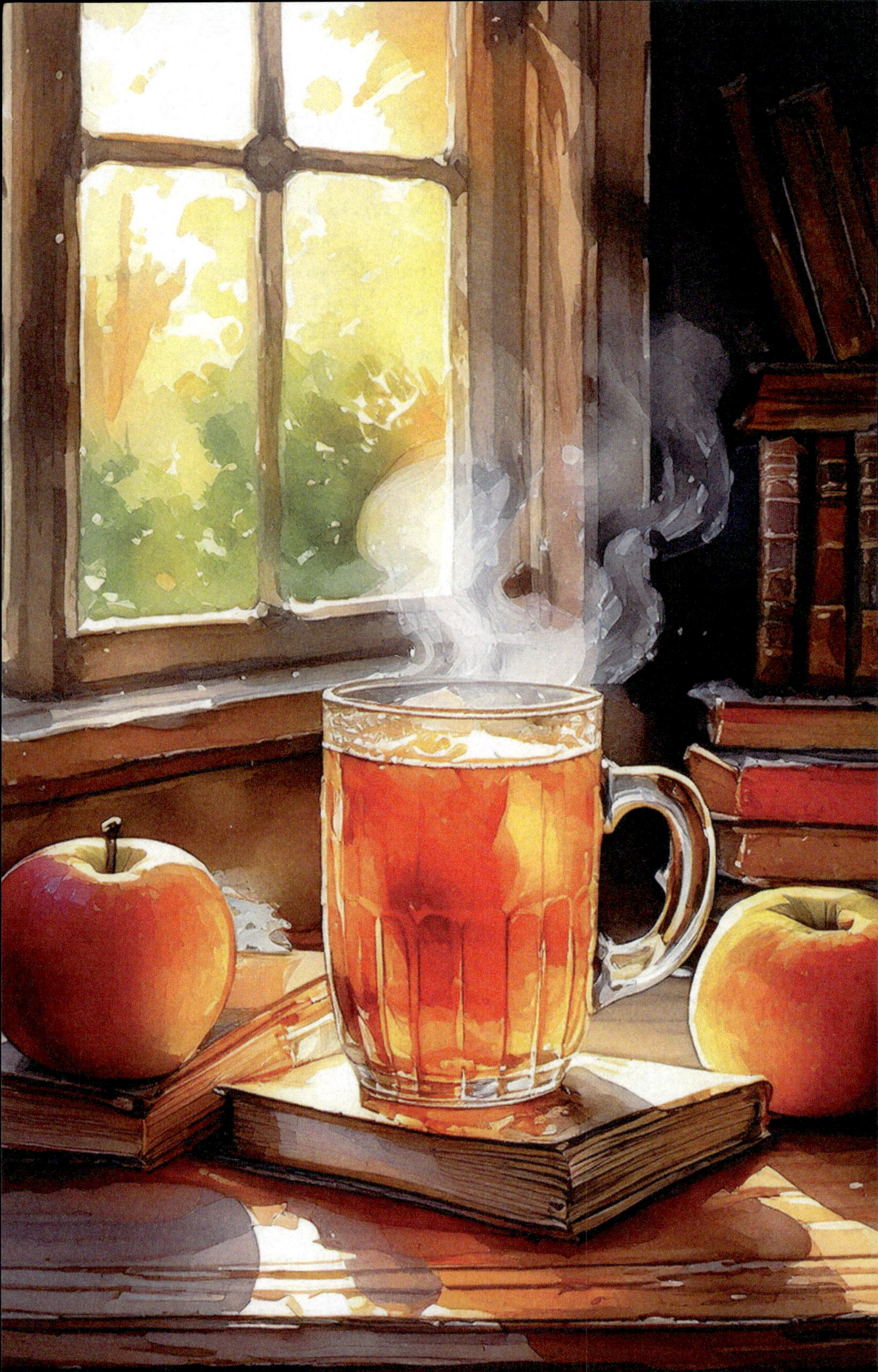

# Warm Apple Cider with Cinnamon

This fragrant drink evokes the coziness of winter evenings in the March home, shared over stories and laughter.

Ingredients:
- 4 cups apple cider
- 2 cinnamon sticks
- 4 whole cloves
- 1 orange, sliced

Instructions:
1. Simmer the Cider: Combine all ingredients in a pot. Simmer over low heat for 20 minutes.
2. Serve: Ladle into mugs and garnish with a cinnamon stick or orange slice.

# Acknowledgments

Creating this cookbook has been a journey of love, creativity, and connection. I want to thank my family and friends for their endless support, encouragement, and feedback throughout this process. To my readers, thank you for sharing in this celebration of Little Women and the warmth of its timeless meals. And to Louisa May Alcott, whose words and characters have inspired generations, this book is a humble tribute to the magic you created.

*Thank you*

# A Note on Victorian Cooking

The recipes in this book are inspired by the traditions and ingredients of the Victorian era, a time when home cooking was a cornerstone of family life. The March family, with their modest means, would have relied on seasonal produce, simple preservation methods, and creativity to make meals special.

While the recipes in this book honor that spirit, they've been adapted for the modern kitchen. You'll find approachable instructions, updated measurements, and accessible ingredients, making it easy to bring a touch of Victorian charm to your table. I hope these dishes offer a glimpse into the heart of Little Women and inspire you to create lasting memories around your own kitchen table.

# About the Author

As both a lover of classic literature and an avid home cook, I've always been inspired by the way food brings stories to life. Little Women has held a special place in my heart for its rich portrayal of family, resilience, and love. This cookbook is my way of celebrating those timeless themes through the lens of food—a universal language of comfort and joy.

When I'm not in the kitchen, you'll find me tucked away with a good book, exploring the countryside, or finding new ways to bring a little old-world charm into everyday life. Thank you for letting me share this journey with you. I hope these recipes bring a touch of Little Women into your home and heart.

*Autumn Rosewood*

Printed in Great Britain
by Amazon